# Foreword

Dear Terri,

I don't know if you will remember me, I imagine you touch so many hearts, that it would be impossible to remember us all! I was the one who cried on your shoulder at the curriculum fair at the First Baptist Church of Trenton last April. Both of our cars quit running that month, my husband lost part of his income due to an insurance hike, and I lost my ability to focus and do God's will. Then I met you, and you gave me your book *Ignite the Fire!*. You asked me to write to you—to let you know how I was doing.

When I took your book home with me, I spent the next week studying it from cover to cover. I read, memorized, highlighted, and made notes in the margins, but most importantly—I prayed. When I finished your book, I was ready to begin homeschooling again. I woke up fresh and early Monday morning and I prayed, "Lord, what do you want me to teach my children today?" His answer was, "How to be a friend." I chuckled to myself and thought, okay, that'll take five minutes. What will I do with the rest of my day? But wanting to be faithful and obedient, I began our school day with my three-year-old son's Awana book, *Ern E. Elephant Made Peanut Butter Cookies for His Friends*. Ethan shouted, "Hey, we can do that for our friends too!" That's all I needed to hear. We put up our pencils and books and headed for the kitchen.

My daughter Olivia was seven, my son Jonathon was five, my son Ethan was three, and my daughter Adelia was almost two. I gave them each a turn in measuring and mixing while we discussed what makes a good friend and how we can be one. As we began baking cookies, I shared with my children my favorite Bible story of all—Elijah and the first angel food cake. I told them how Elijah feared for his life, how he ran away and prayed that God would kill him—he'd had enough and didn't want to go on anymore. He lay down to sleep and an Angel came. "All at once an Angel touched him and said, 'Get up and eat.' He looked around and there by his head was a cake baked over hot coals and a jar of water. He ate and drank and then lay down again. The angel of the Lord came back a second time and touched him and said, 'Get up and eat, for the journey is too great for you.' So he got up and ate and drank. Strengthened by that food, he traveled forty days and forty nights until he reached Horeb, the mountain of God" (1 Kings 19:5-8).

So you see—the Lord provided strength to Elijah with the first angel food cake: We had a wonderful time in the kitchen that day.

When our cookies were all finished, we prayed that God would show us who needed a friend. We would take some cookies to them. The first thing that came to my mind was how Jesus taught us to take care of orphans and widows. Well I didn't know any orphans but we do have a widow in our church that I had been praying for yesterday, while sharing with her our experiences in home our "cookie ministry"!

It has been four months since I met you, and there isn't paper enough to share all that has happened because of you and your book. Our cookie ministry continues as does our lesson on how to be a friend—a long five minutes don't you think?

Anyway Terri, I just had to share this much with you. You were my angel sent from the Lord—and your book was my cake—it still holds its sweet savor and continues to strengthen me. The Lord touched me through you and even though the journey is still too great for me—I find my peace and strength in the Lord.

Thank you, Terri

In His Love,
Elizabeth Ross
8/29/2000

# IGNITE THE FIRE!

**Freedom
is Real
Education**

Terri
Camp

NOBLE

Vancouver, WA 98685
www.noblepublishing.com

**Ignite the Fire!**

Copyright ©2001 Terri Camp

Published by
Noble Publishing Associates
Vancouver, WA 98685
www.noblepublishing.com
1800-225-5259

Cover illustration by Darlene Schacht
publishanddesign@home.com
http://www.geocities.com/publishanddesign

Cover design by Alpha Advertising

ISBN 1-56857-089-9

**Printed in the China.**

# TABLE OF CONTENTS

## Acknowledgements

Whenever I see one of my books as a finished product, I am in awe. I am not in awe of what I have accomplished, but in all the people who have helped me to get *Ignite the Fire* into the hands of those parents who need the message that is presented here.

Many of those people have sacrificed of themselves so that I could "work." First, my children who allowed me to practice on them and suffered through many days of "Go do your work, I'm working on my book."

I also am so thankful to Steve, my best friend for life, for all those nights of playing with the kids while I sat in front of my computer screen.

For Debi, my 12th best friend, roadie, and person who always points me to the Father, who encouraged me by telling John to tell me everyday that I am creative. I eventually began to believe you Debi.

I must also thank with much sincerity the other half of my 12th best friend. Drew, you took my words and helped me turn out a great book! Thank you so much! And thanks for lending me your wife on many occasions. I can not express to you all that I feel when I think of the work you did for me. My entire being is filled with thanks.

I would be remiss if I didn't thank all of those on the firetime loop for offering me many ideas and encouraging me with your kind words. I can think of several of you but would hate to miss anyone. You are all great!

Finally, a giant hug and thanks for all of my friends in the homeschool chat room on Crosswalk. You guys have made me feel like I am a part of the best support group in the world!

I also want to thank Mrs. Roelfsema, my high school English teacher. You taught me what it was like to love to learn. Thank you for your prayers and support throughout my life.

# Ignite the Fire!

# INTRODUCTION

How does a family go about schooling by "fire"? In Genesis 19:24, God used fire to destroy the cities of Sodom and Gomorra. Why would He use fire to destroy these cities? I am not claiming to have the mind of God here, just drawing some conclusions on my own. The first of those is this:

Fire purifies. When a forest experiences spontaneous combustion, a great inferno rages. But after the smoke settles, new life springs forth. All the old, dead trees are gone making way for newer, stronger, living trees. When God creates the fire, whether through spontaneous combustion or a lightning strike, the forest is purified. But when someone else starts a forest fire, out of carelessness or even on purpose, they risk the fire blazing out of control and destroying everything that comes into its path—including homes, buildings, and even people.

Likewise, we must not be careless with the education of our children. We must be very careful to ensure that *God* is the one starting the fires of purification in them. Even when we are purposeful in our task of homeschooling, we can cause more destruction than we realize.

If I take the approach that my children will learn best if left to their own, I am being careless. Oh, they will learn some. They may even learn a lot. But when their education is guided by their own initiative, a key component in their education has been left out. That component—God—can never be left out of the equation. God has designed each of our children to be a unique creature. They each have passions given them that have been designed for the purpose of their being. If we allow them simply to "live and learn," they may not gain the wisdom to develop those passions and talents on their own.

If we purposefully seek out the "best" curriculum, we again leave God out of the equation. We are following a man-made plan for our children. God did not design our children to be carbon copies of each other. He did not design them all to know the same things, to have the same gifts, to have the same talents or to learn the same way. No, he created them to be needed and to need the gifts and talents of each other. They spend their years at home developing these gifts, passions, and talents so that when they venture out into the world as adults, they will be able to use them for the glory of God. They will have something to offer that perhaps no

> We must not be careless with the education of our children.

> God can never be left out of the equation.

> God did not design our children to be carbon copies of each other.

one else has. Another person will have different gifts to share with them.

The Fire Philosophy of homeschooling bridges the gaps between the other popular philosophies of home education. When you use a complete textbook approach, the child is force-fed his information, rather than discovering it for himself. On the other side of the bridge, however, is the family that uses no textbooks. They expect the child to discover everything on his own. The Fire Philosophy blends these opposite education styles, creating a child that can launch from a base of information into his own personal discoveries and can even journey further than the available resources!

> The Fire Philosophy of homeschooling bridges the gaps between the other popular philosophies of home education

The Fire Philosophy is a proactive philosophy of homeschooling. It requires sacrifice on the part of both mother and father. When people ask you how many hours you homeschool your children each day, you will not have a definitive answer. The Fire Philosophy of homeschooling is a twenty-four-hour commitment, just like being a parent. On the other hand, it frees you so that you do not feel like you are "working" with your children all the time. You can do laundry and homeschool. You can wash dishes, do the ironing, nurse the baby, play with the toddler, teach the seven-year-old how to read, and fry the bacon. You can not, however, sit in front of the television all day long. If you are in the habit of doing that, get out of it now.

> The Fire Philosophy is a proactive philosophy of homeschooling.

It saddens me that many parents choose their curriculum based on how "easy" it is for them. The goal often becomes creating children who can go to their rooms/desks/table and do their "work" on their own. Hey, I'm guilty here. I couldn't wait for my children to read so that they could go off and do their work on their own, coming to me only for correcting, or the occasional question. My goal wasn't for them to love learning; my goal was for them to learn to read so that they could do the daily assignments on their own.

The goal for our children has become different now. *We no longer are looking for them to be able to get their assignments done. We are now looking for them to create their own assignments.* Our goal is for them to understand the concepts they learn. It is for them to know more than just the who, what, and where; the goal is that they may also know the when, the how, and the *why*.

My favorite quote of all time is, ***"Education is not the filling of a bucket, but the lighting of a fire."*** William Butler Yeats.

When I throw a question out to my children like, "What war in Iowa would Winnie the Pooh have liked?" I want them to think about it. When they give up, and I tell them, "The Honey War," my goals are met if they return with the question, "What was that?" If they just say, "Oh," then I have been simply filling buckets with stale information.

A child who has only been filled with stale data and facts will often feel that his bucket is full. He won't want any more. Or worse yet, he may act like the bucket that has been tipped over, neither receiving nor retaining anything.

I want children whose buckets are filled, not by me, but by the ash that remains after the fire. The ash of the fire can only be gathered by my children. I cannot shovel it into them.

*"Education is not the filling of a bucket, but the lighting of a fire."* William Butler Yeats.

Perhaps this illustration will help you understand the concept: Take a great big bucket and put a little kindling in the bottom of it. Strike a match. Now, if you just leave it alone, you have a few ashes left in the bucket. But if your child sees you putting kindling into the bucket, they will begin helping you build the fire. The kindling will not be sufficient anymore, and larger pieces of wood will need to be placed in the bucket. The fire rages. Still more wood is placed on it. Wow, this is fun building the fire! You have to go further into the forest to get more wood. Still you and your companion continue building the fire. When it is time for the fire to go out, you slowly let it extinguish. You wouldn't dare throw water on this fire; the ashes would spill out onto the ground. Often you will be able to create a new fire in another bucket from the fire you are now letting smolder. Or you can even have several fires going at one time. When the fire is out and you gaze into your bucket, you see that the bucket has been, after all, filled with the ashes from the fire.

In the same way, the Fire Philosophy of home education begins with a small flame. Together, you and your child add fuel— kindling, sparks, or logs—to the fire. As the fire glows brighter and brighter, the thrill of building it increases. Digging deep into the forest, your children begin to seek out their own understanding just to keep the flame ablaze. When the fire goes out (and the Lord will direct this timing) the ashes that remain are the permanent knowledge and understanding your children retain. Small flames of enthusiasm in learning provide starter fuel for other flames, in other areas, and the excitement of building the fire ignites a passion for learning that burns brighter with every new discovery. This is the model and metaphor for the Fire Philosophy. If this idea inspires you or if you want your children to grow in their enthusiasm and understanding of your schooling, then read on.

Leonardo DaVinci said, *"Just as eating against one's will is injurious to health, so study without a liking for it spoils the memory, and it retains nothing it takes in."*

I think DaVinci had the right idea. Have you ever met a person who loved pie so much they dreamed of entering the pie-eating contest at the local county fair? Or perhaps it was the root beer guzzling contest, or the ice cream eating contest. Whether that person won the pie-eating contest or not, more than likely they no longer like pie. My husband's friend participated in a Monopoly marathon, playing for twenty four hours straight. Afterward, he swore that he would never again play the game he had once loved.

If you've ever tried to teach a child to read before he was ready, you know what I'm talking about here. We had one daughter who was allergic to reading. She was eating when she didn't need to eat yet. She didn't like it and she retained virtually nothing. We had determined that she needed to read. After all, she was five years old, and everyone knows that five-year-olds *need* to learn to read, especially *homeschooled* five-year-olds. The world is watching us, not to mention grandmas and grandpas. So we pushed. She would sit next to me on the couch and do the book with me. As soon as she had to read the first letter she would begin scratching, coughing, sneezing and even twitching. This went on for a long time. Finally after a few months of her not learning much of anything and continuing to be allergic, I decided to stop teaching her to read. I waited until I could spark her interest. I bought an easy reader book about wolves and told her the book was hers as soon as she could read me the back cover. She then had a desire to learn to read.

Today my daughter claims that reading is her God-given talent. Using the Fire Philosophy, she learned to read and to love it. The Fire Philosophy ignites fires in our children so what they learn is both retained and enjoyed.

## THE FIRE

We have chosen the term "fire" because it so fully incorporates all that we are trying to do with our children. It conveys a sense of excitement in learning, and it invokes the image of a burning passion for understanding.

Beyond just the emotions that the word "fire" conveys, however, its letters also provide a useful acronym for the philosophy itself. FIRE stands for "Freedom Is Real Education." What do I mean by "freedom"? I do not mean allowing our children to have ultimate liberty. I do not mean that we allow our children to play computer games ceaselessly. I do not mean our children are allowed to watch movies, even "good" movies all day long. The History Channel has some great educational programs on it, but it will not teach our children to think and grow for themselves. Instead, it will develop in them a passive learning process. An occasional show or two will not harm them, but if it becomes your habit to "see if there's something good on," your children are missing out. Never watching anything is better than becoming educational vegetables.

The freedom that I refer to is a freedom that comes only from following God: "Now the Lord is the Spirit and where the Spirit of the Lord is, there is freedom" (2 Cor. 3:17 NIV).

The fifth chapter of Galatians begins, "It is for freedom that Christ has set us free. Stand firm, then, and do not let yourselves be burdened again by a yoke of slavery" (NIV) Verses 13 through 15 say, "You, my brothers, were called to be free. But do not use your freedom to indulge the sinful nature; rather, serve one another in love. The entire law is summed up in a single command. Love your neighbor as your self. If you keep on biting and devouring each other, watch out or you will be destroyed by each other."

What does this mean for me in light of homeschooling? It means that my yoke has been lifted. Christ has set me free from my burdens. As a homeschooling mom trying to follow a standard curriculum, I found myself bound. I found myself burdened. It wasn't until I gave up our homeschooling to Jesus, that I once again found that freedom.

I often found myself wanting to study a certain area with my children, but I felt confined by the books I was using. I felt like I was

> FIRE stands for "Freedom is Real Education."

> 2 Cor. 3:17: "Now the Lord is the Spirit and where the Spirit of the Lord is, there is freedom."

> It wasn't until I gave up our homeschooling to Jesus that I once again found that freedom.

giving them more work in what was an already overloaded day. I was struggling with the promptings of the Holy Spirit in my life. He would prompt me to study a certain area with the children, and I would reason that there just wasn't enough time.

Now that I am first turning to the Lord, I find the promptings from Him get done. It's a great feeling knowing that your children are learning what the Holy Spirit wants them to learn.

Take note though—verse 13 holds a serious concern to keep on guard against. We are not to use our freedom to indulge the sinful nature: rather, serve one another in love. One aspect of that sinful nature for a homeschooling mom who is educating her children through "FIRE" could be laziness. I urge you not to become lazy in educating your children.

One of my favorite groups of verses is Deuteronomy 6:5-9: "Love the Lord your God with all your heart and with all your soul and with all your strength. These commandments that I give you today are to be upon your hearts. Impress them on your children. Talk about them when you sit at home and when you walk along the road, when you lie down and when you get up. Tie them as symbols on your hands and bind them on your foreheads. Write them on the doorframes of your houses and on your gates."

Those verses illustrate education by "fire" the best way possible. We are not to set aside a certain amount of time for educating our children. We are to be educating them all the time.

I know some of you are saying, "But the Bible isn't talking about algebra. It is talking about God's Word."

The Word is the foundation of your homeschooling. If it isn't, it doesn't matter how much algebra you are doing. Everything our children learn should be learned in light of Scripture. If all scientific concepts were taught in light of Scripture, we wouldn't have a whole group of Christian children who aren't sure if evolution is true or not. Scripture would be the foundation, and science would simply build upon that. We are instructing our children upside down. It doesn't matter if you give your twenty minutes of Bible first. That is not giving God's Word priority; that's simply giving it required time. God wants us to live in freedom. To do that we must live God's Word: We must "walk" in His Word, "get up" to His Word, and even "sit" with His Word. Remind yourself frequently what Deuteronomy 6 says: "Impress them on your children. Talk about them when you sit at home and when you walk

---

**I urge you not to become lazy in educating your children.**

**Deuteronomy 6:5-9: "Love the Lord your God with all your heart and with all your soul and with all your strength. These commandments that I give you today are to be upon your hearts. Impress them on your children. Talk about them when you sit at home and when you walk along the road, when you lie down and when you get up. Tie them as symbols on your hands and bind them on your foreheads. Write them on the doorframes of your houses and on your gates."**

**The Word is the foundation of your home schooling.**

along the road, when you lie down and when you get up. Tie them as symbols on your hands and bind them on your foreheads. Write them on the doorframes of your houses and on your gates" (KJV).

Freedom in the Fire Philosophy of homeschooling is giving our lives up, giving our children up, and giving our time up to Jesus. He enables us to walk in freedom, when we are slaves to Him.

Now that we know what freedom means, what is a "real education"?

I went to Webster's 1828 dictionary to find out what he had to say about the word "real." This is what it said: "True; genuine; not affected; not assumed. The woman appears in her real character."

If "real" is to be defined as that which is true, we therefore need the definition of "true": "Genuine; pure; real; not counterfeit, adulterated or false; as true balsam; the true bark; true love of country; a true Christian."

The definition for true has a great bearing on the definition of real. Real means True.

—The *true* light which lighteth every man that cometh into the world (John 1:9).

**EDUCATION**, n. [L. educatio.] The bringing up, as of a child, instruction; formation of manners. Education comprehends all that series of instruction and discipline which is intended to enlighten the understanding, correct the temper, and form the manners and habits of youth, and fit them for usefulness in their future stations. To give children a good education in manners, arts and science, is important; to give them a religious education is indispensable; and an immense responsibility rests on parents and guardians who neglect these duties.

A real education is one that encompasses more than just reading, writing, and arithmetic. A real education is an education that seeks to know what is true. It is not passive. It is proactive. Filling out a workbook is passive. Discovering the truth about gravity is proactive. Newton was being proactive when he developed his theory about gravity. He may have seemed to be passive (just sitting under a tree), but he was thinking and seeking for truth. In fact, he was being educated as he sat under the tree.

I once heard a story of a young boy on his way to manhood who came home to be homeschooled. His parents apparently knew the

Freedom in the Fire Philosophy of homeschooling is giving our lives up, giving our children up, and giving our time up to Jesus. He enables us to walk in freedom, when we are slaves to Him.

A real education is an education that seeks to know what is true.

benefits of the Fire Philosophy of homeschooling. He did not have any interest in doing his bookwork. All he did was stare out the window. His parents decided to allow this passiveness for a time. That young man was not *just* staring out the window. He was observing his environment and actually became an expert on birds, which later became his passion.

A real education is an education that is not rooted in a workbook or a textbook. *It is an education of the mind.* It is an educational process that allows God to use the child's mind to develop the passions that God Himself created in that child.

A real education is an education that relentlessly seeks after truth. A child does not merely accept as fact all that is given him. He observes and discovers for his own what is true. This can only work if the child is rooted in God.

What I often hear, and have even spoken myself, is that there isn't enough time to "do Bible." We fill our children's days with too much if there isn't time for Bible. Also, you cannot "do Bible." Oh, yes, you can sit at the table for twenty minutes, read a chapter or two, memorize a verse, and say you have "done Bible." But that is *not* rooting your children in God. God must be the focus of your life. He must be the One who decides, guides, transforms, and educates your children. When He is the guide behind the education of your children, they will be able to come to a real education. Only when He is *the fire* that your children put their faith and trust in, will your children fully realize their passions and talents.

Until your children are totally relying on God to educate them, however, you must be the one relying on Him. You must be keenly aware of what God is doing in the lives of your children. You set the example, you follow His leading, you forge the path, and you set them in the narrow way. Just how exactly you go about finding God's path for your children's education…is a topic for the next chapter.

> A real education is an education that is not rooted in a workbook or a textbook. *It is an education of the mind.*

## *GATHERING THE WOOD*

In 1 Kings, Elijah calls out to his God to light the fire. I too, call out to God.

This is the first step in moving your family toward the Fire Philosophy of homeschooling. As a family, you must surrender your children's education to God. I know you're saying, "But how is God going to teach my children grammar?" Well, isn't He big enough? Didn't He create everything? Does He not know every-thing? Give Him your children, and He will light the fires that need to be lit to ignite the passions within them.

I call the following step, "gathering the wood." If you are trying to start fires, it is vital that you begin with good wood. If you are using the world's standards of measurement, you are using green wood. If you are using God's standards, you are using wood that is perfect for burning. If you light a fire under a child and the wood is not good, it will simply fizzle and go out. We could gather all the sparks and matches we want, but without good wood, it will profit them nothing.

### The Fuel Book

I will encourage you now to get a notebook (from now on called the "Fuel Book"). Choose a notebook that feels good to you—you will be using it frequently. Whether it's a three ring binder, a spiral notebook, a small spiral, or a hardback journal doesn't really matter. You can even decorate it if you want.

With your Fuel Book, a Bible, a pen or pencil, and a locked door, sit down with the Lord. If your husband is a guiding force in your homeschool, pray with him. If you can't do this now, find a time alone when you can. Please do not read the next chapter in this book until you have been able to do this first step. Don't move forward one step until you've had the chance to pray.

### Tending the Fire

I'm not going to tell you what to pray, but I can give you some guidelines that have helped us to be focused and to be within the will of God.

I will use the ACTS model for prayer.

Adoration—Acknowledge the sovereign power of God. Tell Him how much you love Him, Etc.

Give Him your children, and He will light the fires that need to be lit to ignite the passions within them.

**The Fuel Book**

Please do not read the next chapter in this book until you have been able to do this first step. Don't move forward one step until you've had the chance to pray.

**C**onfession—Confess that you have not been giving the home educating of your children to Him. Confess to Him that you have been allowing others to educate your children. Whatever confessions you need to make, make them now. For some of us (me included) this may take quite some time.

**T**hanksgiving—Thank Him for loaning you His children, for they are only on loan to us. Thank Him for each child, by name.

**S**upplication—Ask Him to guide you step by step. Ask Him to take over educating your children. This would be the time to get specific. Ask Him what you should study as a family. Listen to His voice. So often when we pray, we talk and talk and talk, and then we hang up. Prayer is a communication, a conversation. Conversations are two-way. *Listen.*

When God is talking to you, take notes. It's okay to pray with your eyes open and pen in hand. You might try asking for specifics for each child while you do this. As things come to mind, write them down. They may be personal, spiritual, academic, or perhaps all three at one time.

You may also hear a sermon that makes you think of something you would like to be working on with your children. You may read something in a book that seems particularly important. Your child may say something to you which causes you to "take a note" that you want to come back to later. Your Fuel Book should become a part of you. Take it everywhere you go, just in case you want to write down a message from God.

You can organize your Fuel Book anyway you want. I recommend putting tabs in with the name of each of your children on the tabs. You might even have a tab for your family as a whole. A lot of education in our home is done with everyone together, including Mom and Dad.

Here is an example from David's page:
- Begin concentrating on the social graces of being a man: opening doors for Mom, bringing in the groceries, caring for his sisters, etc. [David is eight years old.]
- Find interesting books for him to read. Concentrate on the sciences as the main topic. Biographies of Christian scientists would be great.
- Encourage memorizing math facts. Spur him further when he comes to me with a math conversation. [David will often come to me with some great mathematical discovery. I could

let his discovery end there, or I could spur him on to a higher level.]
- Give David pages of poetry to copy in his notebook. Encourage him to read them and recite them out loud for the family.
- Encourage David to read out loud to me. Repeat what he has read, then have him read it again. Have him try to read the sentences as a whole, rather than word by word.
- Give him experiments whenever I get them through E-mail, or other places.
- Encourage David to spend time in his Bible. GET DAVID A BIBLE!

This reminded me that I hadn't bought David his own Bible yet. Last year he wasn't reading with any fluency, but now he is. He needs to have a Bible of his own.

Having these pages helps to keep me focused. I usually just add to the list, but sometimes—like if I felt David had mastered his multiplication facts—I will cross it out. You can also use this as a base for your record keeping.

Having a separate record book for each child's work is a good idea. You could have a separate page for each of the topics from the page in his Fuel Book. The first page of his record book would say, "Begin Concentrating on the Social Graces of Being a Man."

record book

On the page about social graces, you would write things like, "I stood outside the van door for three minutes yesterday, waiting for David to open it for me. Today, I only waited for one minute. I saw progress in David's kindness to his sisters." I like to keep the notes on these pages positive, but if the child isn't getting it, that should still be recorded in the Fuel Book.

One good way to organize the personal record book is to separate it by subjects that you work on. This way, you aren't rifling through page after page trying to find the one that talks about reading biographies.

The next page in David's record book might say, "Memorizing Multiplication Facts." You might write, "2/26/98—We played the floor game today. David only missed two facts, both sixes. Will continue working on sixes, but he seems to have the threes, fours, and fives down pat."

You don't have to record in this everyday. But they tend to learn a lot even when they aren't officially "doing school".

In order for this system to work, you must spend time with your children. You simply cannot be an absentee mom, waiting for your child to come to you with great insights. It is okay for your child to go off and be alone, but you should always be aware of what he is doing and even be engaged with him on a regular basis while he is doing something alone.

If your son or daughter goes off to build a rocket ship, you need to peek in on him or her occasionally. You might need to offer some assistance, or perhaps point the child in a certain direction. You might need to help add fuel. You might need to call Daddy at work. Hopefully you do not need to call the fire department. Or, you might need to be there when an experiment fails. We need to learn to be sensitive to the needs of our children. Consider this "tending the fire."

## God's Standards

I want to encourage you to not settle for what the world has to offer. The world's standards for our children are not the same as God's standards. God's standards are much higher. The world doesn't care if we are raising spiritual leaders. The world doesn't care if our children love the Lord with all their heart, soul, and mind. The world doesn't care if our children have a greater love for their fellow man than for themselves. If the world doesn't care about the things that are most important to us, why do we measure the success of our children based on the world's standards? People may use the term "measure up," but the unit of measure is far below where we want to be.

When you are writing in your children's Fuel Books, use the system of measurement that is the highest. Do not base your ideas on the standards of the world. When we allow God to be in control, the standards we've had for our children will rise dramatically.

I'm going to give you two examples of standards for Ashley. The first one will be using the world's standards as my base measurement. The second will be using God's standards. (Ashley is my oldest daughter, currently thirteen years old.)

### World's Standard:
Be sure she does her lessons each day.
Teach her to use a calculator.

---

*In order for this system to work, you must spend time with your children.*

*We need to learn to be sensitive to the needs of our children. Consider this "tending the fire."*

*The world's standards for our children are not the same as God's standards. God's standards are much higher.*

Read thirty minutes each day.
She should be socially adept. Put her in many social functions,
particularly functions with many children of the same age.
It's important for her to be able to CONFORM.

## God's Standard:
Hide God's Word in her heart. Meditate on it day and night.
Ashley now owns her own bread-making business. She should
learn good stewardship—budget, save, and give. She will be
responsible for all the record keeping required. She may hire
brothers and sisters to help her if needed.
Ashley will read great works of literature. She shall spend much
of her leisure time reading about great men and women.
Help her to not be peer dependent.
Train her to be HOLY (Romans 12:2).

Do you see the difference?

It is important for us to know the difference between God's standards and the world's standards. If we are educating our children
to fit into the world, we are falling way short of where God's
standards lie.

As you are praying for your child, do not pray with the world's
standards in mind. You can pray that God will give you the tools
and guidance needed for your kid to have a high SAT score. And,
I am confident that He will, if that is your goal. But, wouldn't you
rather pray that God will give you the tools and the guidance to
help your child to have a heart for God, to develop the passions
that God has given him for His purposes, knowing that this means
a superior knowledge?

God has created each of our children to be different. Therefore,
we must turn to Him and allow Him to show us what, where,
when, and how to teach and instruct our children.

We all want the best for our children, which is why we must turn
to the One who has the best standards.

After you've had your initial fireside chat with God, you may
then read the next chapter.

It is important for us to
know the difference
between God's standards
and the world's
standards. If we are
educating our children to
fit into the world, we are
falling way short of
where God's standards
lie.

We all want the best for
our children, which is
why we must turn to the
One who has the best
standards.

## THE OXYGEN

Every fire must have oxygen in order to continue to burn. Even the very smallest spark must have oxygen. You, the parent, need to view yourself as the oxygen for the fire. You are an essential component in the Fire Philosophy. Sure, you could release your child to burn on his own, but without the oxygen there—praying, encouraging, lifting up, and offering some helpful suggestions— the fire would go out quickly.

What does it take to be good oxygen?

It takes dedication to your children. You must be dedicated to uplift them, to pray for them, and to "be there" for them when they need assistance or guidance. You must also be dedicated to stay out of the way when they need you to.

To be good oxygen we need to have strong relationships with our children. We need to know what makes them tick. We need to be ever watchful for that spark in their eye, which can turn into a raging fire if given the oxygen to burn.

So, how do we act as the oxygen for our children?

One way is to know the different ways children learn. Some children are tactile learners. They like to touch things. If you are teaching a tactile child how to read, you might cut the letters out of sandpaper so he can feel them. Others are auditory learners. Hearing information is the best way for them to process information to their brains. The visual learner will be fairly easy to teach how to read. But getting them to remember dates that you have read to them will be a little trickier.

Neurophysiological studies have proven that more factors are involved than just a child's predisposed learning style. These factors include temperature, sound, light, and even food intake. Some children learn better when they can sip on water; some learn better with music on and others when it is totally quiet.

I'll never forget a time when a grandmother called me in despair. She had begun homeschooling her grandson and he wasn't able to sit at his desk and read to her for the thirty minutes she was requiring of him. After talking with her for a bit, I discovered that her grandson enjoyed curling up on the couch with Grandma, having cookies and hot chocolate. I told her to try reading with that environment the following day.

> You, the parent, need to view yourself as the oxygen for the fire. You are an essential component in the Fire Philosophy.

> To be good oxygen we need to have strong relationships with our children.

She called me the next night, and boy, was she excited! They had made cookies, got the hot chocolate, curled up together under the afghan on the couch, and he read to her for almost an hour!

Cynthia Tobias wrote a wonderful book called *The Way They Learn*. This is a must read for parents who are implementing the Fire Philosophy of homeschooling.

Try to incorporate as many learning styles as possible in the education of your children. This will have a two-fold effect. First, they will be able to function at their optimal level because they'll be learning in harmony with their learning style, in harmony with the way God made them to learn. Second, it will give them exposure to the other modes of learning, making them more rounded learners. When children are exposed to learning in all the various modes, they receive each style in doses small enough to handle.

When you take a hands-on learner, for example, and thrust him into an environment that is mostly auditory, he cannot learn as much as he could if he were allowed to "feel" what he is learning. You can, however, use both philosophies at the same time. Let's say you're doing a unit on flight. You've chosen a great book to read to your children. All the information they need to know is in the book, so you plan to read it, and then give your children a test to see what they have learned. You will be surprised when the tests are turned in and one child appeared to learn nothing. I know what it's like to spend time and energy teaching something to my children only to have them appear to know nothing when it comes time to take the test. But if the tactile child constructs a model of the first Wright Brothers' plane while you read, he will retain more. Now, I know that this is difficult for some of you "I-can-only-do-one-thing-at-a-time" people. But some children simply *must* be doing something in order to absorb what's going on around them. That is the nature of the tactile learning style.

Other children would be so absorbed in doing the model that they would hear muffled sounds in the background, not even noticing that you are reading a really great book to them. As parents trying to teach more than one child at the same time, we must discover what is the best learning environment for each of our children.

I have often thought that with eight children I would eventually get two that are the same. I have not. Yes, there may be just four learning styles, but within them are multiples of combinations. So your job as an educating parent is to *learn your child*. This is not

Try to incorporate as many learning styles as possible in the education of your children.

an easy task, but it is also not impossible. You simply need to do your homework first.

There are many experts in the area of learning styles. Seek them out and discover.

The Fire Philosophy of homeschooling works for a variety of children with a variety of learning styles. I want to remind you, however, that the Fire Philosophy of educating your children is God directed/parent following/with child input. It will not work if any of those three things get out of order. If you are allowing your child to direct, that puts God following or merely allows Him input. God must direct. Please do not forget that. Read Proverbs 3:5,6.

As we are homeschooling our children, we need to view our family with the goal in mind that we are to glorify God first and foremost. That is our chief goal in life and in education. We cannot separate them.

One of the greatest advantages of homeschooling is the enhancement of family unity. I've heard parents say time and time again that when they brought their children home, they became a family once again.

Because of the desire to promote family unity, we do many of our subjects or units together as a family. Daddy cannot always be in on every subject, but he is often in on the decisions of what we will study next.

We often will have meetings, though no one really calls them "meetings," discussing the different subjects the children would like to study. We will often come to the meeting with ideas already. For example, we decided that whatever we were going to study next needed to have a lot of geography. We also wanted it to be missionary related. So, when we came to the meeting, we had already been directed to the mission field. All we needed was some input from the children on what mission field would be interesting. The vote was unanimous for South America.

In this meeting they got excited about the prospect of studying South America. We were the oxygen that fanned the flame. As we talked about some of the exciting things we would learn about, they became more excited. They couldn't wait to begin. We want to be sure our children grasp that they aren't going to simply

---

*So your job as an educating parent is to learn your child.*

*The Fire Philosophy of educating your children is God directed/parent following/with child input. It will not work if any of those three things get out of order.*

*As we are homeschooling our children, we need to view our family with the goal in mind that we are to glorify God first and foremost.*

stand back and soak up information. When we study a geographical region, the children go on a trip to the place we're studying. When we study an historical time period, the children are thrust back in time. If we study a famous scientist, the children watch as he tries one experiment after another. Education is an adventure. As your children learn in this way, they will discover that they desire to go on more adventures.

No matter what you are studying, even if your children are doing individual textbooks, all it takes is a little extra "air" to help fan the flame. If there isn't even a hint of spark in your child, just add some extra oxygen and it will come.

Oxygen comes in at all stages of a fire. It is needed at the point of spark. It is needed as the fire grows and grows. It is even needed when the flame blossoms into a raging inferno.

Sometimes, however, you notice the fire going out. You can see when there is no spark. Sometimes, as we are following the Holy Spirit, it may be time for the fire to be extinguished. Other times, the fire wants to go out, but it still needs to rage a while longer. That is when we must add some fresh oxygen.

Keeping on the subject of South America, let's say you've been studying a couple of countries for a few weeks and the fire is beginning to go out. What do you do? You want to do a little bit on each country but the kids seem to think, "You've studied one country, you've studied them all." Here's one suggestion: tell them that within one of the countries there lies a hidden treasure. You, the oxygen, figure out which country has the hidden treasure. You can hide it anywhere. Each day, give a clue or two as your children explore different countries, trying to find the hidden treasure.

I'll spell it out for you a little bit more. You have decided that the hidden treasure is buried deep within the Amazon jungle of Ecuador. You give the children clues: "An indian chief holds the treasure in a special place. The hut is as long as a basketball court."

You don't tell them that it's in Ecuador; you don't tell them it's the Auca Indians; you just tell them that an indian chief is holding the treasure. As you give them clues, they discover that it isn't in the country that they've studied for the past few days. They will go on to the next country, and the next, until they get to all the

> Education is an adventure. As your children learn in this way, they will discover that they desire to go on more adventures.

> a hidden treasure

countries. Then, they will add up the clues you've given them and discover that the hidden treasure is the Gospel of Jesus Christ. It's hidden in the heart of the Auca indian chief, the same chief who ordered the killing of four missionaries.

As you are playing this treasure game, you may find that one child shows a particular interest in the mission work. You may see that child's heart beat faster as you talk of the tribes that have not yet heard the Gospel of Jesus. You may see tears forming at the thought of those who are lost and dying. You may even have one of your children that stands up and says, "I want to do THAT!"

**DON'T IGNORE THESE SIGNS!** Don't push them under a rug. Don't hide them under a bush. Encourage them. Oxygenate them. (I didn't even make that word up!) This may be their calling; and if you don't oxygenate, they will be missing out on an opportunity to begin working toward their God-ordained purpose.

> *This may be their calling; and if you don't oxygenate, they will be missing out on an opportunity to begin working toward their God-ordained purpose.*

Helping to develop passions within your children is one of the greatest rewards of parenthood. Aside from my children knowing the Lord, I cannot imagine anything greater than seeing them develop their passions, using them for the glory of God.

As parents we can do many things to help fuel their passions. When our children are growing and developing, one of the advantages of homeschooling is that they have more opportunities to explore the world around them. They also have the opportunity to participate in the fields they want to go into. If your child would like to be a lawyer, homeschooling allows you to provide him with opportunities to see a lawyer "in action." You also have opportunities to talk with lawyers. Perhaps they will even allow your child to work in a law office to see what goes on behind the glamour of the courtroom.

What our children want to become is based on their perception of the occupation. In reality, the occupation they are choosing may be nothing like they thought it would be. I once heard of a study that found an astronomical amount of college graduates not working in their chosen profession. Once they got there, they didn't even enjoy the type of work. What a shame that is.

> *Another big advantage of homeschooling with the Fire Philosophy is that our children aren't forced to be "carbon copy children."*

Another big advantage of homeschooling with the Fire Philosophy is that our children aren't forced to be "carbon copy children." In other words, we do not seek to make all of the children fit into the same mold. They are allowed to spend the majority of their time on the gifts and talents which the Lord has given them. A lesser amount of time is spent on the things they need to learn to "round" them out. For example, our child who has a gift in mathematics is allowed to pursue knowledge in that area. While they still need to learn the rudimentary skills of the English language, they are not required to spend most of their time learning skills that are not even related to their field of study. Of course they do need to be well rounded, *but not at the expense of their true gifts.* I firmly believe that if we allow them the time to work on their passions and not fill their lives with the unimportant things, we will have young adults who know their place in God's plan, who will work their hardest to accomplish their goals for the Lord Jesus Christ.

Understand, however, that playing video games is considered neither a talent nor a gifting. Some parents would say that if left "to their own," their child would choose video games or television all day long. These are not passions! These are passives! You could even go so far as to call them "snuffers"—the little things that are placed on top of candles to make the fire go out. As a parent following the leading of the Holy Spirit, your job is to eliminate the snuffers and to oxygenate the passions.

Furthermore, let your children see the passions that *you* have. Allow them to see you working at the passions that God has given you. Talk with them about His purpose in their life. I can guarantee that if you oxygenate their passions, you will not need to give them a course on self-esteem. They will have God-esteem, which is far superior.

Many moms come to me and say, "That's all well and good, but it's *my* fire that needs to have some oxygen." That's when I tell them to study something they find fascinating. If you've always wanted to study constellations (but just haven't found the time because you're too busy working with the children), do a study with all the children on that very subject! You will enjoy it. Your enthusiasm will increase. Your children will see that it is desirable to want to learn about different subjects. They will also learn that it can be fun. Perhaps you could do a study on what really happens to socks between the feet and the clean clothes pile. I've always wanted to know that. Haven't you?

Of course they do need to be well rounded, *but not at the expense of their true gifts*

As a parent following the leading of the Holy Spirit, your job is to eliminate the snuffers and to oxygenate the passions.

Let your children see the passions that *you* have.

# THROW ANOTHER LOG ON THE FIRE

When you have a fire going, you can boost the flame if you have some good logs to throw on it. Really big logs will help the fire to rage even longer. When I think of "logs" in educational terms, I think of certain things that are foundational to the education of our children. These things must not be neglected.

The foundational logs of education math facts, good vocabulary skills, good grammar, the ability to spell with ease, and basic facts in several subjects (like the periodic table in Chemistry).

What are the foundational logs of education? They are math facts, good vocabulary skills, good grammar, the ability to spell with ease, and basic facts in several subjects (like the periodic table in Chemistry). And what foundation is complete without a thorough understanding of the Bible? The logs for the fire are extremely important. There may be some people who will tell you it doesn't matter if your children know their facts, but I will contradict them. It does matter.

"Fire Drill."

There are many good ways to teach your children these basic facts. Not all memorization has to be dull and boring. Children don't have to sit around begrudgingly memorizing their facts. Some of my children have even gone so far as to say, "Oh Mom, can't we memorize something today?" You can even make it more fun by calling it a "Fire Drill." Memorization can be done, it can be done well, and it can be done fun.

Memorization can be done, it can be done well, and it can be done fun.

If you notice that your children just don't have their multiplication facts down, take a week off and play with them. Take the time to play some games that will help to reinforce those math concepts and encourage them to *want* to learn their math facts. You could buy some fancy shmancy computer program, but isn't it more fun to get down on the floor and play with them yourself?

the floor game

Have you ever heard these words from one of your children: "Oh boy, I'd better go study my sixes, I don't have them down very well yet." Think that would never happen in your house? I can almost guarantee it *would* happen if you played the floor game.

The floor game is a giant game board played on the floor, or even outdoors. You design the board, you design the contents, and you *are* the playing pieces. (For ease of explanation, I'm going to use multiplication facts.) Get several large sheets of paper, and cut them in half. Have your children write out the multiplication problems on sheets of paper, one problem per sheet. You could use existing flashcards, but having the children write out the cards emphasizes it just a little more. One sheet will have 5 x 1, another will have 5 x 2. Now, make up some special cards—like, "Hop forward two spaces," or, "Go back one," or even, "Go back to the beginning." The neat thing about this game is that you not only get to make up the cards, but you also get to make up the rules.

We made one big die out of posterboard. You could have two dice if you want or even use a little bitty die.

When we play this game, I lay the cards out in serpentine fashion around the house. We go up the stairs, down the stairs, into the bathtub, around the wet towels (these are the hazards), and to a final "end spot."

(Another advantage to the floor game is that the children will delightfully run around cleaning up the living room if they are going to be able to play the floor game—just an added bonus that all moms would appreciate!)

Before you play, decide the penalty for a wrong answer. We used homemade family trivia cards. A wrong answer on a problem is met on the next turn with a family trivia question. If they get that right, they may then advance on the next turn. If not, they must answer a new family trivia card.

Let the play begin. All children participating will roll the die (or dice). The highest number goes first. If you would like to play this with all ages, adjust the game accordingly. Just put two numbers on the sheet, and, depending on their age, they either have to multiply or add the numbers. We choose to play separately for adding and multiplying.

Let's say the first child rolls a five. He walks five cards. He must answer the fact or do what the card says. If he answers correctly, he may roll again. If you have one child who is going to answer most of them right, you might limit how many times they may roll. The greatest joy with this game is in its flexibility.

Another game you can play with multiplication or addition facts is the penny toss game. This also works for phonics drill.

The penny toss game works like this: In each cup of a muffin tin write either a number or a letter. For phonics drill, put letters into each cup. Mark off a starting line and have the children toss pennies into the cups. When they get a penny into the cup, they must correctly say the sound that the letter makes. If they say the

the penny toss gai.

sound correctly, they get to keep the penny. About the most this game will cost you is twenty-five cents per child. I can usually handle that. One problem you will run into when playing a game like this is that the older children will want to play too. What I have them do is form words, either four, five, or six letter words, based on the letters that are in the tin. It isn't as easy as it sounds. But they line up for hours and do not tire of this game very quickly. I tire faster than they do.

**color-coded memorization**

Suppose you want your children to memorize the books of the Bible. Not only do you want them to learn the books, but you also want them to learn the order of the books. One way to do this is to use color-coded memorization. Purchase some sheets of felt and cut them into horizontal strips about an inch and a half to two inches high. The first five books will all be written on the same color of felt. You can choose the color based on something you want the children to relate to the books, or you can simply group them. If you use tan for the first five books, you might explain to them that tan signifies the tan sand as the people wandered through the desert. Either you or your children will write one book on each strip of felt. When you're done, you'll have five books on five pieces of tan felt.

Place the felt pieces on the floor, or the couch, or somewhere they will stay put. Cover a small Ping-Pong ball or a plastic golf ball with Velcro. The object of the game is to hit the books of the Bible in order. They must throw the ball at the first book, Genesis. If they hit Genesis, they may try for Exodus, and on and on. Again, you decide the rules. If they miss, you may make them place all the books they've earned back in place, or you may let them keep them, allowing the next person to begin where that one left off. Eventually your children are throwing the ball at sixty-six books in the proper order. You might even sing a book-memorization song as you play the game.

Some children will learn something more solidly if it is color coded for them. Remember the visual learning style? If you want them to learn all the states and their capitals, you might want to use color coding for the different regions. This will help some children to retain the facts better.

**Scrabble.**

Another log, a strong vocabulary, will be useful throughout their lives. One of the games you can play to help build a stronger vocabulary is Scrabble. In our home, we allow use of the dictionary to find words they want to place on the board. This helps them to learn new words, so we've made it a house rule. If you come to our house to play Scrabble, my children will be looking up words in the *Official Scrabble Players' Dictionary*.

In The Dictionary Game, one person looks up a word and says it out loud. Each of the players writes down a definition for that word, including the person who chose it. The definitions are scrambled and each person votes for the one they believe is the right definition. The winners each get a point. Play advances to the next person.

The Dictionary Game.

A third way to improve vocabulary is to have the children each secretly choose a word to use throughout the morning. They should use it in sentences that make sense, of course. At lunchtime, everyone tries to figure out what each person's new word was. If the word is discovered, then both the person who used the word and the person who discovered the word may get a treat at lunchtime.

secret word

Still want more ideas for vocabulary improvement? Buy each of your children a dictionary, punch a hole in it and tie it around their waists! I'm just kidding. I do, however, purchase a dictionary and a thesaurus for each child and encourage him or her to use them.

One more vocabulary building game is The Dictosaurus Game. Mother chooses a paragraph and writes it on a white board, or on something similar. The goal is to be the one person who—using a thesaurus or a dictionary—can change the most words in the paragraph. The paragraph could be anything Mom decides. Let's say I want to use the nursery rhyme, "Jack and Jill." I will write out, "Jack and Jill went up the hill to fetch a pail of water," etc. The children then write out the rhyme, "Jill, along with Jack, hiked to the peak of a knoll, with the purpose of acquiring a container filled with clear liquid from the well." You may require your more advanced students to rhyme the second line with the first. Children love to be challenged.

The Dictosaurus Game.

When I was growing up, my dad, my sister, and I played the Dictosaurus Game using common clichés, and we thought it was great fun. In fact, we still talk about playing that game.

Still want another vocabulary building game? Begin with one word, like "aardvark." The first person says, "Aardvark." The next person must add a word to aardvark that begins with the same first letter. So they may say, "Arty aardvark." The next may say, "Arty aardvark advances." And on and on it goes. We do, however, allow the use of conjunctions to help advance the sentence or story along.

spelling bees

To encourage your children in their spelling skills, have spelling bees with them. Get the official spelling bee lists and play Spelling Bee Competition. This game will be more fun if you give different words to the kids based on their skill level. Don't give the six-year-old a word like "unpretentious," unless, of course, he can actually spell it. Sign that child up for the real spelling bee competitions!

3 x 5 cards

For younger children you can write all the letters, plus some duplicates, on 3 x 5 cards. Give them a time limit and have them organize the letters to form as many words as they can. They must, however, be spelled properly. Another game for younger children uses the same 3 x 5 cards. Two players each draw seven cards. With those seven cards they each form a word. The first child may make the word "deck." He then draws four more cards. Every two-letter word earns two points; a three-letter word earns three points, etc. There is an advantage in being able to play multiple cards from your hand. Play until all the cards are gone, then they add up the scores. This is one of those games you may find your children playing for hours.

These are just a few ideas that I have accumulated over the years to help my children with their "Fire Drills." These logs, when used as the foundation of a good fire, ensure that your children will be able to build fires that rage for a long time.

# S.P.A.R.K.S.

## Sparks Promote an Attitude that Releases Kinetic Studies

What does that mean? Basically a "spark" is a plan, idea, or project that promotes in your children a desire to study a subject, or promotes in them a desire to improve the skills they have already attained. It will produce in them an "energy" (that's what "kinetic" means) which makes them *want* to continue to learn, explore, and study. Once your children get the hang of the sparks concept, they may begin inventing sparks of their own. You do not have to be creative to come up with sparks for your children. Steal them from other people. Whenever you hear a mom talk about a spark she used to ignite her children, write it down and use it! Keep track of sparks in your Fuel Book. Not all children will be sparked by the same things. Notice what things inspire *your* children.

All of the sparks listed in this chapter have been tested on real live children. (No children have been harmed in this study.) The age levels vary, of course, depending on the abilities of each child, but the neatest thing about sparks is that the child will either create or expand from wherever he is. A five-year-old and a ten-year-old beginning with the same spark will learn, will grow, and will both be challenged.

Let's begin with some sparks for you to try on your own children:

One of the best sparks to begin with is a **mailbox**. Don't go out and buy a new mailbox from the store. Have each of your children make their own personal mailbox out of shoeboxes, tissue boxes, oatmeal containers, etc. They may decorate the boxes anyway they want. My children's boxes even have flags on them that can be raised when the children have mail. Allow them to have their mailboxes near their bedroom door, hanging from the wall, or placed on shelves. Please understand you must set up a couple of rules. A letter placed in someone else's mailbox must be encouraging, uplifting, and kind. This is not a time for Big Brother to tell Little Brother that he's a pain in the neck! Packages are allowed too. Mom and Dad might need to get in the act and have their own mailboxes!

This simple little mailbox has been known to help children learn to spell better, because they don't want to send a letter to Dad

> Basically a "spark" is a plan, idea, or project that promotes in your children a desire to study a subject, or promotes in them a desire to improve the skills they have already attained.

> **Mailbox**

with misspellings in it. It energizes them to write, write, and write some more. Children learn to communicate effectively from having a personal mailbox.

You remember making valentine boxes at school, don't you? Mailboxes are a similar concept, but the children keep them up all the time.

**science experiments**   Easy **science experiments** are another great way to put a spark in your child's learning. Simple science experiment books are available at all the major discount stores. There is even a scientist who will e-mail a science experiment to you each week. (If you would like an experiment a week, e-mail Robert Krampf at krampf@krampf.com) He also travels around the country, a great opportunity for you to take your kids to see a "real" scientist. These experiments are great ways to begin your week. Your children will often find experiments they would like to do on their own.

**floor game**   The **floor game** is a spark I discussed in the chapter on Fire Logs. I added it here too because it is such a valuable spark that I want to make sure you don't forget about it. Let your children decide what floor game they would like to play and what they want to learn about. Perhaps they are studying a continent and would like to plot a floor game with the countries, traveling around answering questions about them. Don't forget that your children are often a wonderful source of sparks.

**Velcro ball game**   The **Velcro ball game** was also discussed in the Logs chapter. Again, let your children figure out what kinds of things they want to learn. This is a great game for an older child to do with a preschooler. They could cut out different shapes and place them around the room. The child then tries to hit the shapes the older child has shouted out.

**older children teaching younger children**   Speaking of **older children teaching younger children,** this is also a spark. We have some time set aside in our schedule for the older children to teach something to the younger children. Our oldest will work with a younger child on phonics, or she may read to all the younger children. We have so many children in our house that they are grouped into older and younger children. I often wonder how the younger children will feel when they are thirteen years old and we still refer to them as "the younger children." Another one of our older children does an art lesson with the younger ones. This is a great time for all of them and gives the older children an opportunity to share a talent or gifting with a younger child. If you do not have any younger children, borrow some from another homeschooler for an hour or so each week. A young mother with only young children will probably appreciate it if you bring them to your house for an afternoon of playdough, paint, or other messy craft.

Another opportunity I'm including as a spark is **volunteer work.** You could have one of your children volunteer for a story hour at the library. Reading aloud is a marvelous skill of prime importance that is often overlooked. Boys and girls alike should be able to narrate a story clearly. You might decide to volunteer as a whole family.

**volunteer work**

Do you all know what **roll end paper** is? It is the end of the rolls of newsprint. Many newspaper offices will sell hundreds of feet of this paper for a dollar or two. Not only is it economical (we make our own wrapping paper), but it is also a great spark. If you unroll some of the paper, your children are *going* to find a use for it. If you are studying the human body, outline each of your children and have them draw the parts of their body. The little ones will draw in major things like eyes, ears, etc. The older ones may draw the nervous system, or the organs, or even draw and label the muscles.

**roll end paper**

Another project you can do with roll end paper is to tape it on the wall and let your children write notes or draw on it. This may even be a keepsake for you someday.

We homeschoolers often hear about the importance of **timelines.** Not only are they great for your children to get some historical perspective, they are also great for sparks. When parts of your timeline seem bare, your children will want to fill those spaces up. There are many ways to make timelines, and there are also books on timelines. We once used roll end paper to make a timeline, using ten inches for every decade. That timeline was like a scroll. We had a great time working on it, but didn't use it as much after the initial few times because it was so big and heavy. It was about fifty feet long. Was the experience worth the time and effort we put into it? I believe it was.

**Timelines**

We have children who are competitive. We believe that healthy competition is good. Therefore, we use **contests** to help spark our children. All I have to do is announce there will be a contest and everyone races for the resource books. I usually just outline the contest for them, tell them the rules, and send them on their way.

**Contests**

My children especially like when we have contests with the other families in our homeschool group. One time we had a contest to see who could create a vehicle whose main passenger was an egg. The vehicle had to travel down a ramp, crashing into a board, without breaking the egg.

**Nature walks**
**Nature notebooks**

**Nature walks** are a must. Have your children take a few things with them when they go on a nature walk. **Nature notebooks** are vital. My children keep a backpack already packed for the days I tell them we are going on a nature walk. In their backpacks they carry pencils (some carry colored ones) and their nature notebook, which is a small spiral notebook with a hard back. The sheets are blank at the top with lines on the bottom. They also have observation books in their backpacks.

**Biographies**

Reading **biographies** is one of the best sparks I know, opening new interests for my children. I will discuss this at length in the Fire Books chapter.

**family games**

One way to give your children an appreciation of their own family heritage is the development of **family games**. Have your children create games for grandmas and grandpa, or aunts and uncles, etc. You can create a game like "This is Your Life." Include some of the historical things that happened during that person's life or have your child interview the person they are creating the game for and include some of their "stories." You may even include trivia from their life. That's just one way to create a family game.

**board game**

Whenever I see my children getting a little bored with a subject, I have them create a **board game** based on the subject we are studying. All I do is furnish them with poster board. They create the rest.

**Encyclopedia Roulette**

Another fun and easy game to play is called **Encyclopedia Roulette.** I instruct each child to get an encyclopedia. They all sit down and I tell them to look through their encyclopedia for a certain amount of time and find something interesting to share with the rest of us. We then vote on the most interesting topic. Or, I might tell them to all turn to the same page number. They must then peruse the page and tell us all what their page is about.

**famous person**

Have your children dress up like a **famous person**. They will then give a speech based on the life of that person. The other children or audience members will try to guess who your child is portraying.

Have your children create a **Jeopardy-style game** based on anything they want. The contestants of the game … will be Mommy and Daddy!

Sometimes you can use a **movie** to spark an interest in a child to learn more about a certain time period or a certain person in history.

I have found, when we decide on a **unit for the whole family** to work on, that the children get more excited than if they just do something on their own. If we are all working together on it they are more apt to want to discover information to share.

**Treasure hunts** are a great way to teach map making skills, geography, history, etc. All you have to do is have a treasure to hide and a way to find it. You could do treasure hunts throughout the house. Or you can do giant treasure hunts outside. You can create a giant map and have your children go to the correct places. You can even tell one of your children to create a treasure hunt, and off they will go.

We found a spark that has lasted for a long time when one of our children created their own personal **Web site**. She spends a great deal of time doing research and working on her Web site. She set the goal to make it educational and informative and is constantly revising it to provide more and more information. This was a spark that lighted a fire for her, a fire that may never go out.

We like to have **tea parties** at our house. You may think a tea party is frivolous and could not possibly have the ability to spark a child. Oh, but that is not true. We like to read poetry during our tea parties. Often a child will create a poem on his own that he would like read at the tea party. Some children look forward to teatime with great excitement. And who wouldn't want to sit around drinking tea (or Kool-Aid), eating scones (or animal crackers), and reading delightful poetry?

Often if I want to encourage some creative writing, I will **assemble a book** and give it to the child. Or, I might just tell the child to assemble a book and write a story. They love to do this! I assemble the book placing blank paper between two sheets of cardstock. I then three-hole punch them and bind with yarn.

Another way to spark an interest in writing is to have them **corre-**

**Jeopardy-style game**

**Movie**

**unit for the whole family**

**Treasure hunts**

**Website**

**tea parties**

**assemble a book**

**Corredpond**

**Food**

**puppet show**

It's not just the external difference you will see, but also deep within them, they will be developing a desire to learn.

**spond** with someone who writes neatly and who is faithful (Grandma) to return letters. This helps them to see how important it is to have neat handwriting (and has the added benefit of sparking a good relationship with Grandma).

I often use **food** sparks for my children. You can make a bunch of pizzas the same size and cut them into wedges to help teach fractions. You can make a batch of cookies, cut them into state shapes, and have the children make a relief map of the United States with frosting. You can even have an international food day, based on the region that you want to study.

Do you have a **puppet show** theater? I think all homeschooling families should have a puppet show theater and some really good puppets. All you have to do is set up the theater in your living room, and the kids will take up the puppets and begin.

You will see as you begin implementing a spark just how energetic your children can get when they are excited about learning. They will run to the encyclopedias. They will bounce to learn their multiplication facts. They will even jump to find the right resource that they need for a project. It's not just the external difference you will see, but also deep within them, they will be developing a desire to learn.

## *ADDING THE KINDLING*

On a few occasions a spark will go out after just a couple of minutes. Then I need to come along and add a little kindling to get more out of that spark. In this chapter I'm going to expand on some of the sparks discussed in the last chapter. Sometimes we want to do too much for our children. We often need to ignite the spark and leave our children alone to develop a raging fire on their own. But there are also times when it takes the children a little longer to learn to make their sparks burn. You can then turn to this chapter to add some kindling. Or perhaps the spark was raging, but the fire has gone out, but you want to light it again. Then you can use some of the ideas in this chapter to "jump start" the spark.

We'll start with **mailboxes**. A few weeks or a month after your children have made their mailboxes, they may stop writing letters to each other. This is when you slip an anonymous gift for them into the mailboxes. Leave one for yourself too, so the kids don't catch on! If that isn't enough to get them to begin using their mailboxes again, start leaving clues to some information. In the letter ask the child to respond by 5:00 the next day with the correct answer to the clue. You might give them a treasure for answering the clue. Some of the clues could be related to something you've been studying. Or you might tell them to write you a letter using a list of words. This is a great way to give them "assignments." They won't even know they are getting assignments; they will just think they are having fun!

We have had little visitors over who enjoyed seeing our children's mailboxes. When this happens, our older children will often make a mailbox with the visitors so they can take a mailbox home for themselves.

**Science experiments** don't usually lose their spark if you do a new one each week. It's important, however, for Mom to remain diligent in doing the experiments *with* the child. Nothing gets rid of the spark faster than a mom who doesn't have the time to do the experiments with her children.

Have your children create observation notebooks. They can record in the notebook each experiment and what they discovered. Have them first write what they think will happen in the experiment (their hypothesis!). You could prompt them to try other experiments. Don't forget that they need to do the experiments at least three times so they can check their data.

**mailboxes**.

Our older children will often make a mailbox with the visitors so they can take a mailbox home for themselves.

**Science experiments**

There is nothing that gets rid of the spark faster than a mom who doesn't have the time to do the experiments with her children.

If you are a mom that isn't especially diligent when it comes to science experiments, create a folder of them to be taken out any time the child says, "Mom, I'm bored."

**observation notebooks**

Additional kindling could be to buy your children kits based on some of their interests or something you are studying. We bought a volcano kit to help kindle a study we were doing. If you have a young child who is interested in the way things work, you could buy them a resource book on the way things work, a computer program, or give him things to take apart. When my son received the book *How Things Work*, he wanted right away to build a type-writer. So we let him try to figure out how he would do that. And don't forget the power of Legos to capture the mind and encourage creativity.

**The floor game**

**The floor game** deserves one more mention, as it is such a wonderful way to learn information. One way to add kindling to this firestarter (which probably doesn't need any kindling added to it) is to have the children each develop their own floor game. You can also use flashcards that you already have. If you have a deck of U.S. Presidents cards, you can use those as your game spaces. You can even make the floor game a little more physical. You could have spaces that require them to move in a certain way. For example they may encounter a space that directs them to slither from then on. Or perhaps they must hop. Or maybe they must crab walk. This adds additional fun to the game.

**teaching a younger sibling**

If you have a child that balks at the idea of **teaching a younger sibling**, have them teach something that is very special to them. Instead of having them teach a child to read, you might have one of your children who is gifted in music teach a younger sibling the piano. Or perhaps a child who especially likes to cook could have a young assistant help her in the kitchen. You could even have a craft time led by an older sibling.

**Volunteer**

One way to bless your neighborhood is by having your children **volunteer** to help neighbors with a project. Perhaps an elderly neighbor needs to hire someone to shovel the walk. This would be a good way not only to help your children, but also to help those around you. You could have someone in your house volunteer to shovel without pay. You could even expand this a little and illus-trate to your children the idea of budgeting by showing them how much a person would receive from a fixed income like Social Security. I can almost guarantee your child would be more than willing to sacrifice his time to help. Another volunteer idea is to go to a local nursing home and perform a puppet show for them. You could even have your children go to a nursing home and read to those people who can no longer read. Prepare some songs and go sing to them. There are many opportunities for service that we need to be aware of and need to make our children aware of. Sometimes the child may just become a special friend to another person.

I was a young girl of about seven when I began "visiting" my dear friends, the Darzees. They owned a bakery in town when we first moved to their area. I would go over to the Darzees' house a few times each week. Whenever I went, I was allowed to sample one of the products from the bakery. I will never forget the taste of those wonderful plumped up sugar cookies. They were my favorite. Mr. Darzees would talk to me of Greece and would teach me some Greek phrases. This prompted me to want to please him so I went home and learned the Greek alphabet. I can still say it for you if you'd like me to. I never did learn to say it backwards, but I did try. I even tried translating some of the New Testament in Greek based on a book that my dad had on his bookshelf. Later in high school I participated in a unit study of Ancient Greece. When in college, the first class I signed up for was Greek. I acquired much of my teaching style from great men like Socrates and Plato.

So you see, volunteering to be a friend can have lasting rewards and can spark fires that rage forever. I am convinced that one of the people I will be allowed to visit with in Heaven will be my dear friends, the Darzees. Perhaps their mansion will be across the street from mine.

**roll end paper**

Adding kindling to the **roll end paper** may seem a little silly at first. When the children get into using the paper, however, there is no stopping their imaginations. I like the roll end paper particularly for drawing the human body, but it has a lot of other uses as well. Children could make murals with it. They can draw cities and countries. They can create landscapes. They can use it as a backdrop for a play they are making. My children use it to make huge welcome signs or Happy Birthday cards. It also makes great wrapping paper.

**Timelines**

You can make **timelines** for just about anything you are studying. One way to do a timeline is to put a long strip of paper all around your room. Make it high enough so little hands don't pull it down but not so high that the children cannot add to the timeline.

Having a timeline up at all times is a very good idea. Just put up a different one if you want to do a different period of time. You could even make it very elaborate and color code it. Perhaps you will make all the government figures and information in red. You might do the music and drama in yellow. Inventions might be in blue, etc. If you are studying the Revolutionary War, you might have a timeline just for that. Whenever you talk about another event or battle, just put it on your timeline.

**Contest**

Of all the times I've announced a **contest**, I don't remember ever having to add kindling to the spark. However, there have been times that we have needed to "go back to the drawing board." There are times that a child's "invention" just doesn't work. It is sometimes difficult to keep them from being discouraged, but if you make it a little less painful by saying something like "back to the drawing board" in a cheerful way, it may keep the discouragement away.

Our recyclables are items we've collected that would normally have gone in the trash, but we figured they might be useful for something, someday

In our basement we have a room that my husband calls the utility room. But the rest of us call it the arts and sciences room. In there we keep all the paints, a drafting table, painting sponges, glue, glitter, etc. We also have our recyclables in there, items we've collected that would normally have gone in the trash, but we figured they might be useful for something, someday. This is the stash the children use to make many of their projects. We put two garbage cans in our kitchen. Into one we put the normal garbage. Into the other, we put things like paper towel tubes, toilet paper tubes, clean juice cans and lids, styrofoam trays (do not use any that have contained raw meat), etc. You can also pick up supplies at garage sales. Or, just let it be known you want garbage, and people will happily collect it for you.

Whenever your children get that glassy eyed look of boredom, announce that you are going to have a **contest**. I have not found a good source of contests, so either the children or I have come up with most of them. There is always an objective. When we had a boat contest, the objective was that the boat must float, must be able to move through the water, and must not sink if a hurricane came. The children discovered what things were buoyant and what were not. They discovered there must be a certain amount of weight. The boat contest was one of my favorites.

**science fair**

Another type of contest could be having a science fair. Arrange with another family or your homeschool group to get together and do a science fair. It doesn't have to be elaborate to be great fun for all of the children.

If it were feasible, I would take my children on a **nature walk** every single day. When I was reading the biography of C.S. Lewis, I discovered that he did take nature walks every day. These were some of his most loved times. I want that for my children. Not only am I facilitating in them a love for learning, but I am also trying to instill in them a love for God and for His creation. Taking daily (or as often as you can) nature walks will help keep them on this path. There is surely delight in relishing in the beauty of nature. The children also receive the added benefit of spending uninterrupted time with Mom. When out on a nature walk, the child does not have to compete with telephones ringing, dishes that need to be done, or any of the other things that seem to be pressing in on Mom.

Different mediums of art add fun to a nature hike. One day, you might take with you some charcoals, another day, watercolors, and still another day, you might take colored pencils or crayons. Don't forget the cookies—they go great with paint!

I will often give my children an assignment when we get to the trail that we are going to take. Sometimes I will tell them the first person to identify a living plant will receive a reward. Or perhaps, the first to find a creature will be rewarded that day. As we are walking along, it is nice to stop in a particular spot and begin to draw what we see. So often we spend our lives running to the next place and miss the view along the way. I want my children to learn to stop and see all that God has given us. I don't believe life is a series of steps that must be arrived at; it is a meandering trail that simply must be absorbed.

After reading a **biography** to your children, discuss ways in which the life of this person now affects your lives. Whenever I read a biography, a portion of that person's life becomes a portion of my life. I have read many biographies of people who have lived in the countryside of England. I believe this has influenced my own life. As I read of them taking their walks and spending time in places like Oxford with the spires and towers, or of watching the rain come down, day after day, I long within my heart to visit such a country. Even if I can only visit it in my imagination, it becomes a part of my life. One of the beauties of homeschooling is that we can send our children to England, France, or Scotland even if it is only in a book. They can read of the great men and women of faith and, through them, gain a deeper knowledge of the Lord they serve.

**nature walk**

Different mediums of art add fun to a nature hike.

I want my children to learn to stop and see all that God has given us. I don't believe life is a series of steps that must be arrived at; it is a meandering trail that simply must be absorbed.

**Biography**

Just as it is important for our children to know of the great men and women that shaped our history, it is equally important for them to know their own heritage.

**family game**

**board games**

Just as it is important for our children to know of the great men and women that shaped our history, it is equally important for them to know their own heritage. This component is often missing in our lives today. When looking at the heritage of your family, you can spark a desire to know more about a country or a group of people. You can spark a desire to want to be a part of your family's ancestry.

My husband's family has a legend that their family came to America via a cabin boy on the Mayflower. The claim is that a boy of twelve left Scotland in 1620, came out as cabin boy on the Mayflower with the Pilgrims, and settled in the state of Connecticut. Our children could create a **family game** based on this piece of information. They could discover more about the Pilgrims. They could learn more about Scotland. The list is endless because each new discovery could lead to another discovery.

Your children can create family games based on the life of an ancestor. My husband's dad has in his possession the diary of a captain in the early 1800s. This relative could easily be turned into a spark for our children.

A relative of my mom's was the first white child born in the county. My dad's grandparents came over from Norway. All of these tidbits can be turned into board games that can be given as gifts and shared with members of the family.

Speaking of **board games**, these are sometimes a little harder for children to begin creating. Sometimes they need some added kindling from Mom or Dad to help them get the idea rolling. Sometimes all it takes is a brainstorming session, but there are other times that they need a little extra prodding along. You might have to help them by giving them assignments. Again, they don't really think they are getting "assignments," but think they are creating a board game.

If they are creating a game on the Civil War, the first thing you might have them do is gather some facts. You might tell them that they each need to come up with a certain number of facts about the Civil War. You might then tell them to find some interesting stories about the Civil War. Have them discover the supplies that the armies needed. The list is endless. Once they gather their data, transfering it into a board game is pretty easy.

**Encyclopedias** are one of the most loved series of books in our house. When our children were very young we began using the encyclopedia to learn about all the things that began with a certain letter. For example, we might have chosen the letter S. We would all (three of us at the time) sit on the couch and look through the encyclopedia (letter S) to find new information. It was great fun and the kids would not let me stop. They would want to keep going through the whole book. That wasn't possible in one sitting, of course!

You might use an encyclopedia as a beginning point for a paper that your child is going to write. If they are stumped with an idea, you could simply say, "Go to page 368 in Volume N, and write about that." It's totally random, and sometimes not appropriate, but it adds a sense of mystery to their paper. Even Mom doesn't know what their paper will be about on that day. There have been many sparks ignited in just this very way.

There also comes a time when a child grows beyond the encyclopedia. You know the day when your child comes to you and says, "I want more information than they are giving me." That is the grand day when you drop all of your plans and head over to the library.

Some of you may wonder how you can use a **movie** to spark your child, or what kind of kindling you can add. You may choose a movie based on the idea it will spark your child, or you may stumble upon a spark by accident. This happened with us while watching the movie *Searching for Bobby Fisher*. Our oldest son, who was five at the time, became enamored with the idea of playing chess. His daddy sat down with him that night and explained the game to him. Just a few months later, he was challenging everyone to chess. From then on, he received a chess set for Christmas, and for every birthday and Christmas since (he always seems to lose a piece down the vents, thus needing a new one that often). It's fun for us to find him different kinds of chess sets. We will probably get him a marble chess set when he turns eighteen. His goal was to eventually beat the chess master (a.k.a. Daddy). It took him three years, but he finally did it. It was a day that will forever be etched in his memory.

We have used other movies hoping they would light a spark in our children. Many of the movies we chose were historical or biographical in nature. We have found that, for the most part, this is an effective way to light a fire.

**Encyclopedia**

**a movie**

**Encyclopedia**

Still need kindling for a movie? Try having your children construct one of the sets (in miniature), or paint one of the backdrop scenes from the film. If the film is historical, have the children write a story about one of the characters taking a time machine to the modern day. What would they say? What would they think of us? If they are adventurous enough, your children may enjoy acting out one of the scenes from the movie. They might even want to act a conversation between one of the characters and someone in modern times. These are just a few ideas. If you take the time to discuss the movie, other ideas will come as well.

**unit study**

When the whole family is involved in a **unit study**, I have found the children get into it more than when they are doing things alone. If you really need a little more incentive, have them invite some friends or relatives over, and give a little presentation about what they have learned.

One of the fun ways to do a unit is to all sit down and decide what you are going to study. Then choose a day that you are all going to come back together and discuss what you have learned. The object is to try to come up with some interesting facts that aren't known by anyone else. Or a child can create a crossword puzzle or other kind of "test" and administer it to the entire family.

**Website**

To help a child want to learn more about a subject that they are interested in, assign them a **Web site** to create. Many places on the Web offer free home pages. They also offer point and click Web site creation, which is not the most beneficial for a child. One of the biggest benefits of Web site creation is learning to write HTML and Java. I think it is important for them to learn these skills. We checked out a book on HTML from the library and our children were off to a running start. There were also tutorials on-line that I allowed them to look at. I will caution here that I will never allow my children to search on their own. My oldest is thirteen right now and still has not been allowed to randomly search. Perhaps in a few years I will allow it with a safe search engine, but otherwise, I doubt it.

**tea party**

When having a **tea party**, it would be delightful for you to invite one of the widows from your church. (This would also encourage the children to clean the house, although I'm sure none of you have any trouble getting your children to clean!) Another benefit of inviting a widow to tea is the company of an older member from your church. Often the homeschooling family is misunderstood. This is a great way to be a shining light, even to the people in your own congregation.

**Book**

If your child has trouble writing their own **book**, you might start with them drawing the illustrations and narrating the story to you. Sometimes the process isn't nearly as daunting if they don't have to write the book out in long hand. You might at first need to give them some ideas to write about. For some reason, writing a book about their life is a lot more fun for my children than writing a paper.

**Food**

If you have never used **food** to spark an interest in your children, you have been missing out on a special blessing. Pizza is an especially fun way to learn. You can make pizza relief maps using chicken, sausage, various vegetables, and ranch dressing. You can color the ranch dressing blue for water, brown for desert areas, etc. The mountains could be a pile of chicken topped with some ranch dressing. Perhaps a patchwork of sausage and broccoli for states like Iowa and Nebraska.

Whenever we are studying a new region we try to find foods to sample. It might cost a little more to buy a plantain, but the memory alone is worth the cost.

Being able to educate our children has multifaceted benefits. Among those benefits is an education where the children actually learn what they are studying. Whereas so many attempts at education dampen the desire and dull the understanding, sparks and kindling keep the embers burning for years. The memories that we make with our children as we study with them enrich everyone in the family. As we all work on a project together, we create a bond with each other that gives our family a solid and lasting base on which to stand.

## FUELING THE FIRE WITH NOTEBOOKS

What is a notebook, and how can it be used to help fuel fires in your children?

A notebook is a three-ring binder. You can purchase any size that you want. I like the one-inch size the best, as I find them easier to store on a shelf. I also prefer the kind with a clear pocket on the front because your child can design his own cover, and, later, the notebook can be used for something else. You need to have plenty of these, as the children will each want several of their own. Equip each notebook with some blank paper (three-hole punched) and some lined paper. You may want to use page protectors. These can get expensive if you have a lot of "productive" children, so you might consider protectors just for the special projects you are currently working with. For example, if we are working on South America together, each of the children will have a South America notebook. This would include outline maps (in the protector sheet), perhaps some general information sheets, and other information you may want to include. Don't give them too much information at the start, but encourage them to find their own information sources to include.

I have some notebooks that I require, and some that are optional, based on the particular interests of the child. As we discussed earlier, a Creator who knew exactly what He was doing created each child in a unique way.

The greatest advantage to the notebook concept is that children will learn at, and a little above, their individual level. They will be stretched, not held back. One disadvantage of the public school system is that the brighter children often have to wait for those who aren't quite getting it to catch up. This is not the case with notebooks. I would recommend the notebook concept even for the public schools. Parents who are supplementing their children's public education at home could use this concept to encourage their children to develop their passions and learn about the things that interest them. Who knows, they might even be able to use it as a school project sometime down the road.

Many groups can use the notebook concept for many different reasons. My sister and her husband are youth leaders at their church. They require their youth to keep a notebook for the year on the subject of metamorphosis. Notebooks serve as a personal portfolio, recording and organizing whatever investments a person makes into their own education.

*Notebook*

*Many groups can use the notebook concept for many different reasons*

One thing to remember when embarking on a notebook, or series of notebooks, is to have a specific goal in mind. It doesn't have to be an elaborate goal, but it is important to have a defined goal in order to know if the objective is being met. It isn't enough to say, "I want them to learn all they can." That isn't specific enough. On the other hand, having a goal that is too narrow is not a good idea either, unless you have a child that is older and wants to specialize in a certain area.

Without a defined goal, you may find yourself going from one notebook to another without any real content to the notebook. You also may find that you are only touching on the surface of many subjects. If your goal were more defined, you would be delving further. However, if the goal is too narrow, you may find that your children are not searching beyond that which meets the specific goal.

We work on only one or two "required" notebooks each day. We would not have enough time to do each subject justice if it were given only a thirty-minute time slot. I found my children would just begin to "get into it," and then we would have to switch gears and move on to something else. So we now use larger blocks of time.

## The Bible Notebook

Our children each have a Bible notebook. Even the little ones want their own. Our Bible notebook will not be exactly like your Bible notebook. Again, this is a subject that requires a great deal of prayer and a willingness to follow the prompting of the Holy Spirit. If you feel led to do the same thing we do, that is fine—as long as you know what the Lord has called you to do in that area.

Our current Bible notebook is based on the books of the Bible. Each day that we work on these notebooks, we work on a new book of the Bible. For example, the first book is Genesis. Thus the first page in our notebook is Genesis. After the book name, we have a statement that shows the relationship of Jesus in that particular book. The statement for Genesis is, "He is the Creator." The children may fill in sheets behind that first page as long as the information is related to Genesis, or to the statement, "He is the creator."

Everything the children do on that page, and behind that page, is dependent upon that descriptive statement. I only *require* them to

Notebooks serve as a personal portfolio, recording and organizing whatever investments a person makes into their own education.

"Required Notebooks"

**The Bible Notebook**

write the book and the statement. In reality though, the children never stop there. They take these notebooks to church, and if the Pastor makes a statement or reference from that book, related to that subject or not, they can add it to their Bible notebook. Often the children will pick up their Bible notebooks and draw pictures about different stories that take place in that book. Or, they may choose to write about how the particular statement relates to their relationship with Jesus.

You can do this notebook in one of two ways: you can have them write out all of the books with their statements in order to choose the daily book to study, or you can have them all do the same book as you work each day. In the first option, when you tell them to work in their Bible notebook, they can choose which book they want to work with on that particular day. In the second option, everyone in the family is doing the same book on the same day. I like to maximize my time by minimizing my effort. Minimizing my effort means that we are all on the same page. On the other hand, if you write out all the books, they can work in their Bible notebooks any time they feel like they want to. I suppose you could compromise by spending a couple of days having them write out all the books, then during "required" notebook time, tell them all to work on one particular page. You'll discover what works best for you.

Our statement for Exodus was, "He is our Redeemer." I had the children look up "redeemer" in the dictionary to see what it said. We discussed it at length. Cathy and David were both enamored with this particular book and statement. They worked a long time on their Bible notebooks that day. That night when Steve began our devotions at dinner, the subject was "Jesus as our Redeemer." Now Steve did not know what we had done earlier in the day, and I did not know what he was going to do that evening. But, the Holy Spirit knew.

As soon as Steve said, "What does 'redeemer' mean?" Cathy shot her arm into the air excitedly because she already knew the answer to Daddy's question. This was a great day for her.

From the beginning of the world to its end, there is no place you can look and not see Jesus. He is everywhere. He is everything. He is before all things, and in Him all things hold together (Colossians 1:17).

If you memorize Scripture together as a family, you can have a separate notebook for that purpose or you can incorporate it into your Bible notebook. Your children who read their Bibles daily, and who are old enough, can write notes from what they read. If they have enough writing to do, you can have them draw relevant pictures of what they read. If your children take notes on sermons, they can put them in their Bible notebook. You could make a block chart of all the chapters in the Bible, paste it to the back cover, and have the children mark off when they've read them. They will be amazed how quickly they can read the whole Bible if they get into the habit of reading daily, and they will know the constant encouragement from seeing their progress.

I would think it goes without saying, but when your child completes the whole Bible, he should be rewarded, BIG!

## Handwriting Notebook

My children are also required to maintain a handwriting notebook. This notebook contains sample letters and notebook paper. They are required to practice their handwriting in these notebooks. Some children become exempt if their handwriting is already neat. I believe I downloaded the sample pages from the Robinson Curriculum.

## Phonics Notebook

The younger children are required to maintain a phonics notebook. When they make mistakes in their writing, I remind them of the phonics rule that would be appropriate and they write it in their phonics notebook. I may elaborate more with this by having them find other words that would also fit this rule. As they look through their notebooks, they may see a pattern and be able to learn from the mistakes they have made in the past.

## Unit Notebooks

Whenever we do a unit together, the children each maintain a notebook on that unit. They are allowed, yes, even encouraged, to go beyond what we are doing and discover for themselves more than what we are covering. During the first day of a new unit I will tell the children what we are going to be studying and what my goal is for the unit. Sometimes they might, as we progress in the study, like to develop a goal of their own. That is okay for them to do, as long as they keep within the original goal as well. I will often give them a handout or two for their notebook. If it's a

**Handwriting Notebook**

**Phonics Notebook**

**Unit Notebooks**

**Art Notebook**

**Personal Notebooks**

The primary reason the
children do their
notebooks is because
they enjoy doing them.

the county extension
office

geographical region, I will often give them a map or an outline map. I may give them questions that I want them to try to answer as we're going through the study. The unit study notebook is a group project, but individualized by the children.

## Art Notebook

A few times per week I will assign a picture that I want the children to draw. They draw either from another picture, or from something that is around them. These pictures they put into their art notebook. We have several good books that instruct them in art. I will sometimes have them do a lesson from one of those books, or I may have them draw something in real life. My children have always been good at drawing. My theory is that they learn to draw because they have the time to draw. Many children simply do not have the time to do the "extras" that make life more fulfilling.

## Personal Notebooks

Each of the children makes their own personal notebooks. These may be on any subject they wish. The personal notebooks may be the foundation for a project the children are working on, or they may just be for fun. The primary reason the children do their notebooks is because they enjoy doing them. I will often find them working on their notebooks during their free time. They take great pride in their notebooks and enjoy showing them off to everyone who is willing to see them. They take their notebooks with them in the car. They take them outside with them. They sit in their rooms and work on them. They check out books from the library so they can do more in their notebooks.

We have one child who loves working in her notebook so much that the other children accuse her of hogging all the notebooks. She has a stack of ten in her room that she is either working on, or has already filled up. Several of these books are a series on the same subject. It has been neat to watch her work improve from the early notebook days to the present.

One resource we have found to be very helpful is the county extension office in our county. They have many booklets on several different subjects. Our extension office is very pro home-schooling and is more than willing to give us free materials, as well as loan us their science kits for extended periods of time. The booklets they have given us are the ones that are used for 4H projects. The booklets are filled with ideas, and they make a great spark for the children's notebooks. Ashley, for example, has a booklet on horses. She uses this as her foundation for her horse notebook. She has also used her notebook to expand into her Web site creation. Some of the ideas on her Web site came from questions and projects in the horse booklet that originally came from the extension office.

I believe notebooks are the most important tools of home-schooling with the Fire Philosophy. Notebooks give your children a way to record what they learn. It gives them an opportunity to study a subject, keeping their thoughts and discoveries in an organized manner. It allows them a medium to "show off" what they are learning to those around them. And it gives you something to look at on those days you feel like a failure, to prove to yourself that the children are indeed learning.

I believe notebooks are the most important tools of homeschooling with the Fire Philosophy.

## *SMOKE*

If there is a fire off in the distance, what is the first thing you see? You see the smoke.

What is the effect of a *raging* fire? The effect is an awesome column of smoke.

The smoke I'm referring to is the character of our children. We want within our children a character that can be seen for miles around. If my children are mediocre citizens, mediocre Christians, and mediocre parents, I have failed them in their education. My desire is to raise up children who are going to produce awesome columns of smoke.

That doesn't mean they must be on stage, or that we must always make them perform. It means that the character within them is so strong that it will be seen. They don't really have to *do* anything to make the smoke. It should just come from them, and I believe that it will. If we train our children to love learning and to love the Lord, they will rise above like smoke from a raging fire.

We can encourage this in our children. We can encourage them to step out at church. We can encourage them to be leaders in the group. Not all homeschooled children are destined to be leaders, but a great many of them will be called to leadership. We are not training our children to be "cookie cutter kids," but we train them instead to set their own course. (Even our librarian calls home schoolers a "different breed.") Homeschooling gives our children the opportunity to learn how to be leaders in their homes, churches, and communities. Homeschooling with the Fire Philosophy in particular will teach our children how to complete objectives. They will know what information needs to be absorbed in order to complete a task, and they will know where to find that information. We are training them to know what they want and to know how to get there. We are also training them to know the Guide who will take them there.

While our children are young, we are their guides. As we seek God and His wisdom for their lives, He guides us. Gradually, as they grow and mature, they learn from this model. They observe and emulate parents who seek God and His guidance. Someday they will leave our home, they will become parents, and they will need His guidance for their own families.

We want within our children a character that can be seen for miles around

They don't really have to *do* anything to make the smoke. It should just come from them

While I haven't had any of my children go out into the world on their own yet, I've seen plenty of homeschooling children who have. I've also seen mine get a taste of what the world is like. If you will indulge me for a minute, I would like to share some observations that I have about my children in the world.

I must admit I had been fearful that my children would appear shy and withdrawn. But that is not true. Oh, it may be true in some instances, but when it really counts, they are *smokin'*. Along with our daughter, who told us the Holy Spirit had been prompting her, we decided it was time for her to make a public affirmation of her faith. We approached the Pastor who, along with the elders, decided that was okay. In front of our whole church, at the age of thirteen, she gave a marvelous testimony that had the congregation in tears. More importantly, she left a mark on their hearts. She spoke about how God is taking away her worry and about how she is learning to rely on Him, especially for the care of her animals. No one knew that shortly before she got up in front of the church we had discovered that her dog had been shot. Perhaps the smoke coming from her was simply for me. I saw a little girl who just months before had worried over every little thing in regard to her beloved animals. And here she was standing before two hundred people proclaiming that God is in charge of her animals and that He knows when they should live and when they should die. Our entire pew (we take up a whole pew) was in tears, and there she stood with barely a cracking in her voice. I knew in that moment that God was in charge of my daughter and that He would lift her up.

I heard someone come up to our pastor later and tell him, "All the kids should be required to do that."

A few weeks later, someone stood up in church and said, "I was inspired by the little Camp girl and would like to share my testimony."

I'm not saying these things to brag about my daughter, but to boast of the working of the Lord. We were unaware of what the Holy Spirit was doing in the lives of the members of our congregation. It was the Holy Spirit who prompted her to share her testimony. She simply obeyed, and God used our daughter as a means to send smoke signals to our church.

Our prayer for our children is that God will reveal Himself in them, as His power in their lives rises like smoke, pointing to the Father.

I knew in that moment that God was in charge of my daughter and that He would lift her up.

Our prayer for our children is that God will reveal Himself in them, as His power in their lives rises like smoke, pointing to the Father.

A sure-fire way to extinguish the flame of learning in your children is to allow them a great deal of time watching television, playing video games, or using the computer.

## *EXTINGUISHING THE FIRE*

As with all fires, there are ways to extinguish the flame. I cannot think of any legitimate reason to intentionally do this, but I'm including some extinguishers in this book so that you are aware of them and can avoid extinguishing the fire in your children.

A sure-fire way to extinguish the flame of learning in your children is to allow them a great deal of time watching television, playing video games, or using the computer. These are passive activities and will sap your child very quickly of the desire to learn. I know this first hand. In a very short amount of time, my usually inventive children went from being always busy to not knowing what to do. It was horrifying for me to hear every morning, "Can we watch a movie?" They weren't watching "bad" things. They weren't just sitting in front of the TV indiscriminately watching a cartoon network or something. These were decent movies that we had approved. I was very busy doing some things, so I needed them to be occupied for about a week. The movies just seemed the easiest way to do that. Visibly, however, the brains began to slow down. If you don't believe me, shut your TV off for a month and watch the change in your children. They will once again be enjoying life and wanting to learn.

We have never had a video game player in our house, but from what I've heard, they are also big fire extinguishers. I would urge you to use extreme caution if you have these in your home.

Computers are a third fire extinguisher. Sure, there are lots of great programs out there to help your child learn this or that. On the other hand, anything that keeps them from exploring and discovering is not good in large doses, no matter how well they are learning their multiplication facts.

Whether it's from television, video games, or computer usage, the massive doses of instant information desensitize a child's mind. After this dulling effect, children lose the ability to appreciate the struggle *and the triumph* of seeking out information on their own. Encyclopedias, books, and maps become boring since they don't move, dance, and sing for them. As the children grow used to information being fed to them in such active media, it steals the joy from the active pursuit of learning. The biggest danger may be that children learn to be dependent on someone else's talents of presentation, rather than taking charge of their own quest for knowledge.

You can quickly extinguish *all* the fires in your children by not spending time with them. A child left to himself will not flourish. There may be exceptions, but for the most part, I believe children desire and need the companionship of their parents to help fuel the fires within them. Therefore, if you remove that time and companionship, the fires will go out. Or, the fires will be replaced with the kind we *do not* want our children to be exploring. We must sacrifice of ourselves, in order that our children will become all that they are meant to be.

If you have a child that says, "Why?" with any frequency, you will know it is often difficult to constantly answer his questions. It is so very important though, that we take the time with them to help them discover the answers. Even when they have asked what seems to be five hundred questions already, and it's only noon, we must be willing to stop whatever we're doing and keep the fire going. I'm not telling you that you can never tell your child that you're busy and cannot take the time to answer him or guide him right now; what I am saying is that parents need to avoid the point where we don't hear the questions anymore. Pretty soon the child will stop asking the questions. He won't stop because he has all the answers; he will stop because in our own selfishness, we have extinguished the fire in him.

On those same lines, however, we can also extinguish the fires in our children by giving them all the answers to their questions. It is easier to simply tell your child what he wants to know. If your son comes to you while you are in the middle of doing the dishes and says, "Mom, how many legs does an insect have?" you will be helping to extinguish his fire by giving him the answer. It would be far better for Mom to dry off her hands and guide her child to the right book in which to find the answer, than it would be for her to simply say "six." Using insect as an example, if the mother is a firestarting mother, she may guide her child to the dictionary. Here they will together look up the word insect. As they read the definition of insect, the child's eyes light up as the mother reads about the insect being segmented with a head, thorax, abdomen, three pairs of legs, and one or two pairs of wings. As the child gazes at the dictionary, he spies a picture of a grasshopper that is labeled with various parts. The child decides then and there that he would like to draw the picture and label the parts. Look back at the mother standing at the sink with her hands in the hot soapy water. If the mother had simply turned to her child and answered him, she would have been filling his bucket with tidbits of information, thereby quenching a possible ignition.

You can quickly extinguish *all* the fires in your children by not spending time with them.

## CONCLUSION

When homeschooling using the Fire Philosophy, it is important not to leave out the vital components.

First and foremost, we *must* allow God to be the leader in the lives of our children. We must train them to look to Him for all their needs, including their educational needs. Through Him, we will be led in the right direction for our children.

Since God created our children with specific gifts and passions to use in His service, the education of our children should be fanning those gifts into flame. In the Fire Philosophy the notebooks, projects, Fire books, and sparks develop these passions so that our children will better serve the Lord and fulfill the purposes for which God designed them.

Finally, don't forget to pray for your children as you follow the Creator in their education.

It still amazes me when God shows that He is leading our family in the area of education. Often He will use one of our pastor's sermons to drive a point home with us that we have been working on in our homeschooling.

Recently, we had been studying South America. I had been trying to find missionaries in South America for the children to pray for as we studied the countries. I was wondering if the children should write to the missionaries and take the study a bit further. The ideas were running thin, and I was beginning to feel like it was time to put an end to our study. I eventually decided that I wasn't going to do any more after our study was over in a couple of weeks. Then the Lord spoke to me.

I was sitting in our pew at church. Pastor was talking about spiritual warfare and the need to pray for certain regions of the world. He even talked about the need to know geography in order to pray effectively for those regions. He specifically mentioned Argentina. When he mentioned that country, Ashley and I both looked at each other and smiled. She, too, knew that the Lord was asking her to pray for the very country she had been studying. It was obvious to me that God had planned more for our study of South America. I may not know the extent of God's plan. I may not know its twists and turns. But I do know my children's education is better in His hands than in mine.

We *must* allow God to be the leader in the lives of our children.

Don't forget to pray for your children

# Camp Fires!

## *FIRE TOOLS*

As with every profession, we need to have some professional tools on hand. I will seek to explain many of the essential fire building tools in this chapter. Some will be self-explanatory. Others may be covered more in depth in another chapter. All are necessary.

**Bible:** If you don't have enough of these in your home for each child, call me, and I will give you some. As soon as a child is beginning to read, he should have his own Bible. If the Bible is an integral part of your schooling, this may be the book he wants to read first.

**Bible**

**Three-ring binders** (the ultimate fun school!)

**Three-ring binders**

When I asked our oldest daughter what we did that was fun in school, she said, "nothing."

"Oh no," I thought. "How could she think we don't do anything fun in school? I give speeches on this subject." When I asked her, "Well, how about notebooks?" she responded that those don't count. After further investigation I discovered she only counted doing math as "school." All the rest was just fun stuff. She had learned that the word "school" meant sitting at a table with a workbook. "Life" is all the rest of the things we do.

Binders just have way too many uses to be left by the wayside. For instance, you can make a history binder of pictures. When you talk about or read a book about a certain time in history, have them draw a picture that would be relevant. Put these pictures in your history notebook. Eventually your children might draw enough to have multiple volumes on history!

You could also make a geography notebook using postage stamps as your theme. Get a package of postage stamps from around the world, place a stamp on the paper, and then find out about where the stamp came from.

Do you remember the Bible notebook using the "Who is Jesus throughout the Bible" premise?

Allow your children unlimited access to three-ring binders. Let them create what they want, but give them time to work on them.

**Paper:** I think this is self-explanatory, but if not, I will elaborate a little. We buy paper in big boxes from warehouse stores. Better

**Paper**

yet, find a printer who would be willing to give you "junk" paper. They make a lot of it. In the winter months we can easily go through fifteen hundred sheets per month. Paper is simply not a product that I conserve. I allow my children to color and draw, color and draw, and eventually they graduate to asking me, "How do you spell horse?" The whole process just flows naturally from an abundance of paper!

**Composition books:** There are several ways to start a child down the path of writing. Here are some ideas:

1. Have the child write a description for a blind man. Look out the window and describe what you see. Or, try to describe a color, or a smell, or a taste. What does an orange taste like?

2. Give your child a couple of sentences, like this: "I couldn't believe it was happening. Right before my very eyes I was viewing the most amazing thing I had ever seen." Sit back and watch where they go with it.

3. Have your child choose fifteen or twenty words (at random) then have her write a story using all of those words. You could model this idea after the "Mad Lib" concept. Have her give you five nouns, five verbs, and five adjectives, etc.

**Pencils:** I have never found that you can actually have enough pencils. Colored pencils are great too. You can also branch into the artistic pencils for shading and things like that.

**Pens**

**Paper punch:** Of course, when talking about paper punches, I must caution you that they make a great big mess ... particularly in the hands of a three year old. Oh, but the joy on their face cutting little holes in everything! The dots do vacuum up fairly easily ... as long as the air isn't too dry ... but then you could do a lesson on static electricity. So, you see, a paper punch is a multi-function device.

**Markers**

**Duct tape:** I believe the need for duct tape is self-explanatory. I will not delve further into this one. (If you need more inspiration, rent some old episodes of "MacGuyver.")

**Composition books**

**Pencils**

**Paper punch**

**Duct tape**

**Paper towel holders/toilet paper holders:** These are a multiple-use item. Keep them all. Don't throw any of them away. Store them in your arts and sciences room. One thing you can do with them, besides tooting reveille when someone asks a thought provoking question, is make a rain maker. Tape one end shut and poke nails into the tube every 1/2-inch on the seam. Don't poke them all the way through, just to the other side of the tube. Pour in a handful or two of beans or rice, tape the other end shut, tape the nails into place, and there you have a rain maker. These are great if you are doing a rain forest skit and want some good sound effects.

**Juice cans/lids:** Again, these belong in your recyclable materials for creating stuff.

**Poster board:** This has unlimited uses. We made a giant die to assist us in the floor game.

Another use for poster board is to make board games. We had one child make a game like chess, but using animals instead. The pieces moved in relation to the type of animal they represented. A gopher could burrow underground and come up anyplace it wanted. The kangaroo could hop forward three spaces. The sidewinder could only move one space up, but it could move sideways any number, etc.

A more advanced game could also be a present for Grandma and Grandpa. Have your child interview their grandparents. (They may need to interview them several times.) Then have your child create a game that would be like Trivial Pursuit, or Monopoly. My sister made a game called Sweenopoly for us. The game's properties were based on the places we all lived, went to school, or were related in some way to our occupation.

You could also make a game based on a book you've read. You could make a Lion, Witch, and Wardrobe game. The players would enter the game at the wardrobe. Sometimes they might have to return to the wardrobe. One reminder here - you can "help," but don't "do" it. Let your children do most of the creating.

Beyond using poster board for games, one of our children likes to create foldaway scenes to play with. She created a barn with a tub of water, a bucket, some tack, a couple of stalls, a tack room, etc. She did all of this with poster board, glue, tape, and Velcro.

**Paper towel holders/toilet paper holders**

**Juice cans/lids**

**Poster board**

**Books/library card**

**Books/library card:** Make reading to your children a priority. Also, listen to your children. If they don't like the book, don't make them sit through the whole thing. Choose another. And don't forget to put on a good show when reading to your children. Sometimes stop at the cliffhanger. No matter how much they beg for more, be strong. It may pay off when you see your beginning reader trying to figure out what happens next when he reads the beginning of the next chapter himself. I let our children work on their notebooks while we read. Even our younger children have notebooks. They just sit and color in them while I read.

These are some of my children's favorites: *Johnny Tremain, Carry On, Mr. Bowditch, Lucas Whitacker, Apprentice, 20,000 Leagues Under the Sea, My Side of the Mountain, Nothing Is Impossible* (The story of Beatrix Potter)

**Set of encyclopedias**

**Set of encyclopedias:** These do not have to be new. Play Encyclopedia Roulette) Have a red-letter day. The first day it is A day. Go through the A encyclopedia together and find a person, a place, and a thing that starts with the letter A. Have one of your older children make up a story with those three things. Talk about the different sounds the letter A makes. Talk about the different phonograms that have the letter A, or that make the A sound like "eigh." Think of things that start with the letter A. Have A's for breakfast: apple juice, applesauce, applesauce muffins, etc. Make a big red A and hide it in your house somewhere. Cut out a bunch of A's and put them on things around your house that begin with the letter A. For the beginning readers, maybe you could have them find things around the house that have an A in them. For example, chair has an A in it.

**Spiral notebooks**

**Spiral notebooks:** The nice thing about spiral notebooks is they can go anywhere without losing the pages. My kids like to take these in the car and write in them while we go on a trip.

**Material, needles, and thread**

**Material, needles, and thread:** You do not need to go out and buy new material. Just give your children some basic lessons in sewing and let them have access to the material. You may be surprised at what they create. Our daughter began making tack for her play horses.

**Pennies**

**Pennies:** These are great for games and counting. Our twenty-month-old doesn't talk much yet, but one of the few words he knows is "money!"

**Muffin tin:** Play the muffin tin reinforcement game discussed in the spark chapter. Use letters, words, numbers, etc. Just the other day I had a mom tell me that her kids loved the muffin tin game, and that they learned many of their multiplication facts the very afternoon they learned of the game.

**Felt:** In addition to being good for color-coded memorization games, felt is pretty cheap and can be used by children to create whatever their imaginations will allow.

**Velcro:** This is my all-time favorite invention! I buy huge rolls of it. The kids use it for everything from tack for their play horses to clasps on their fold-up scenery.

**Ping-Pong balls:** Play a game to help remember facts or information. To memorize the books of the Bible, write each book name on a piece of colored felt. You might want to group them by color. The Pentateuch might be all yellow. The Minor Prophets might be green, the gospels, white, etc. Place them around the living room and have the kids throw Ping-Pong balls (with Velcro) at the books trying to get as many in the right order as they can. Keep a graph with the number they get right. Let them pick out of the Good Kids Box when they get all the books in order. Let them pick out of the Blessed Kids Box when they better their score.

**The Good Kids Box:** This is a box that we keep stacked with small items like pencils, erasers, Velcro, candy bars, gum, etc. We allow children to pick out of it when they do something extraordinary. If they help another child with their chores, if they clean up a room without being told, if they are working on a specific character trait problem and we see them making progress, etc., all are reasons to be allowed to pick an item. We also have a Blessed Kids Box. This box contains smaller items like hard candies, pieces of gum, etc. They are mostly candies. If a sibling gets to pick out of the Good Kids Box, the other children are allowed to pick out of the Blessed Kids Box because they are blessed to have such a special sibling. At various times I may walk up to someone and say; "I'm sure blessed to have children like you guys." That's their cue that they are allowed to pick out of the Blessed Kids Box.

**Money, cash register and products:** Play store. Even my big kids like to help with this. They can be the managers of the store. Again, you don't have to go out and buy pretend food. Just use the empty packages that you've already used.

| | |
|---|---|
| | **Muffin tin** |
| | **Felt** |
| | **Velcro** |
| | **Ping-Pong balls** |
| | **The Good Kids Box** |
| | **Money, cash register and products** |

| | |
|---|---|
| **Index cards** | **Index cards:** Make your own flash cards. Play Hide the Flash Cards." It's fun to do this at night with flashlights. Hide flash cards around the house and when they find one, they get to say what it is. |
| **Black markers** | **Black markers:** I'm not sure what possessed me to want a supply of permanent black markers, but I have since found them to be indispensable. Oh well, some day I may learn. |
| **Dry erase markers and dry erase board** | **Dry erase markers and dry erase board:** These are great for playing Pictionary, writing messages to each other, drawing, etc. |
| **Roll end paper** | **Roll end paper:** This is particularly fun for drawing your children. We learned body parts by having the children lie down on the paper and we traced around them. Little kids labeled the easy parts (arm, leg, etc.) big kids draw in the esophagus, kidneys, and heart. |
| | **Yardstick** |
| **Field Guides** | **Field Guides:** These are great to take with you on your nature hikes. Some children really thrive on nature. These are a good way for them to learn about the world around them. |
| **Animals** | **Animals:** i.e. hamsters, ducks, chickens, dogs, cats, horses, cows, dinosaurs. While some of these you can own as pets, teaching the children a great variety of stewardship skills and responsibility, others you may have to settle for toy versions. |
| | **Tape** |
| | **Glue sticks** |
| **Nature Friend Magazines** | **Nature Friend Magazines:** The cost is $22.00 per year. You can subscribe to this marvelous Christian magazine for children by sending the money to Nature Friend, 2727 Press Run Rd. Sugarcreek, OH 44681 Or call 1-800-852-4482. |
| | **Scissors** |
| **Jars** | **Jars:** Every kid needs some good insect keepers. |
| **Glue gun** | **Glue gun:** Obviously this is only for older children. Don't give a five-year-old a glue gun. |

**Tape measure:** Who needs workbooks to learn how to measure? Measure their wing span, and then measure their height. How does it compare? Two children will have a ball for hours measuring things all over the house. Give them three or four different measuring devices—a yardstick, a ruler, a tape measure, and a cloth measure.

**Tape measure**

**Cuisenaire rods:** These are a must in our house. We use Miquon Math with our younger children. They often will do thirteen pages in one sitting just because it's so fun.

**Cuisenaire rods**

**Funtivities:** We get these kits from the county extension office. They provide hours of fun.

**Funtivities**

**Straws:** Kids can do a lot of things with straws. Give them a half glass of milk and *let* them make bubbles.

**Straws**

**Tennis shoes:** These are to remind you to take walks with your children. Pack a lunch, some treats, your nature books, colored pencils, paints, paper, collection bags, etc. Have a bag ready at all times so that you can shout, "Get in the van! We're going somewhere!"

**Tennis shoes**

**Car keys:** You can't get in the van and go somewhere…

**Car keys**

**Mathematical Compass:** Have your child draw lots of circles. Then have them draw the radius and diameter. They will be clueless that they are learning. They'll think they're just having fun.

**Mathematical Compass**

**Protractor:** Make a sundial with a compass and a protractor. Go outside at 12:00 and place the sundial. Speaking of sun, build a solar cooker. You might even get some solar cells and build a small (matchbox size) solar car. Have a contest to see whose car wins.

**Protractor**

**Cookbook:** Assign the older children one day to be resident chef. Before shopping day, have them plan the menu and then let them go shopping with you. Don't just let them do desserts—have them plan the whole meal.

**Cookbook**

**Food**: Food is a great medium for teaching a lot of concepts. Make mini pizzas in different shapes—circles, squares, rectangles, and triangles. Cut them into the same number of pieces, six for example. Show the principle of fractions. Pizza is also a great way to help learn geography. Get several different toppings and

**Food**

create a relief pizza map. Pancakes are great for making different shapes as well.

**Balloons**

**Paints**

**Paints:** If you have an assigned place for kids to paint, you will be more likely to allow it.

**Shoe boxes, oatmeal containers, cracker box**

**Shoe boxes, oatmeal containers, cracker boxes, etc.:** (Use for mailboxes)

**Envelopes**

**Envelopes:** My children love making mail for each other. Be liberal with your office supplies.

**Puppets and puppet show theater**

**Puppets and puppet show theater:** We made one out of PVC pipe and old curtains for under $20.00. Have your child interview Grandma and Grandpa or some other friend or relative and then act out their life.

**Plastic sheeting**

**Plastic sheeting:** You can purchase this on a roll from just about any fabric store. Use for state cutouts or other regions/countries, etc. Make a giant batch of cookie dough and frosting of different colors. Make a relief cookie. Require the kids to come up with three or more interesting facts about a state, or whatever rules you come up with, in order to be able to eat the state. Whenever we do things like this, we try to make just the primary colors and mix them to make the colors we want. However, for relief maps it is helpful to have a good brown color to use.

**Map**

**Map:** (Cloth ones work great.) We buy cloth maps at WalMart and at fabric stores. They have bright colors and are washable, which makes them especially nice for under a clear plastic table cover. You can do many things with these. You can post a map on a board with a light between the board. Put pinholes in places where there are missionaries that you know of or have written to. This illustrates how we are to be the light of the world.

Make a Grandmap or a Grandpap and plot where all of your relatives live. Using an atlas calculate how long it would take to get there. Find points of interest along the way. You could even go back generations and find out where people came from and plot where they went. Talking to Grandma, you might find for example that she lived in Chicago when she was twelve and moved to New York City at age fifteen, then to Illinois, then Washington, finally ending in California. Explore (talk with

Grandma). There is a wealth of information in grandparents. It is especially helpful to have a plan when the children interview them.

Each day while having dinner at the table with the map under plastic, locate a state and learn a little about it.

**Globe**

**Globe** game: Have one child locate something on the globe. She then tells the other children what she has found and they try to find it. She might have to give them hints. If they can find it without any hints, it's worth more points. If they need hints, their point value decreases. You could even do this "just for fun."

**Teacup**

**Teacup:** This is an essential component to a well-rounded education. A proper teatime should include a snack (animal crackers are acceptable), a drink (Kool-Aid is fine), and some delightful conversation with a mixture of poetry. This is up to you, of course, but I would prefer to have "tea time" with animal crackers and Kool-Aid than to not have it at all.

## *FUELING THE FIRE WITH PROJECTS*

Special projects further fuel the fire of a love for learning in your children. I will mention many projects in this chapter. There are, however, far more projects than I alone could ever think up. Give your children the option of coming up with some of their own projects. They have great minds—let them use them.

project night

You might begin using projects by announcing that there will be a project night three weeks from last Friday. When we have a project night, we require the project to pertain to the subject we are currently studying. Children will use their talents to customize their own projects. If you have a child that is an auditory learner, they are likely to create a multimedia presentation. If you have a child who is kinesthetic, they are more likely to create a hands-on project. That's okay too. You might set some guidelines, or you might not. I think it's a good idea for the children to have an audience. You could invite Grandma, Grandpa, or other relatives to come. You could videotape it to send to family far away. You could invite the pastor and his wife over. Or, perhaps, you might just want them to do the first few project nights for their dad and siblings. Your children may even decide to work together on their project. That's fine too.

family night

We have also instituted family night. This is along the same lines as project night, except it is on a weekly basis and the projects or presentations are strictly for the benefit of the rest of the family. This is one of the single most inspirational projects we have begun. The children work well into the night on their projects for family night. As each week passes, the projects get better and better.

Web sites

Some of the projects your children work on may be one-time affairs, like one for project night, while others might be continuing projects that they work on for an extended length of time, gaining new knowledge and information as they go along. For example, our children have created their own Web sites. These are an ongoing project. I give them very limited computer time, but the children solve this problem by working on their Web sites through the use of their notebooks first. This teaches them many things. Among the most important aspects they learn is that of planning. They also learn patience.

Often their notebook has a lot more content than their Web page. They therefore learn to prioritize. They also learn that sometimes there is more work than time available to do it.

I have been known to tell the kids on a dreary wintry day to go into the arts and sciences room and create something for me. When we were reading *Carry On, Mr. Bowditch*, I had the children create a ship out of garbage materials. This inspiration launched the infamous boat-making contest that we discussed earlier. They learned a lot by trying out their newly created vessels in the bathtub.

create something

Projects, therefore, inspire good contests. We once held a contest to see who could create a vessel that could safely carry an egg to the bottom of a ramp without the egg breaking. The winner was the one whose vehicle crossed the finish line with the egg intact.

Contests

If your child is doing a biography, it is fun for the child to "play the part" of the person in the biography. When we studied the Vikings, our Ashley dressed in a fur coat and made a sword, a helmet, and some meager armor. We also purchased red dye for her hair so she could really be Eric the Red. It was memorable!

play the part of the person in the biography

Of course, dough is a marvelous project medium. You can make salt dough maps. One daughter recreated a famous Revolutionary War battle. She made the ocean, many English soldiers and American soldiers. She painted their clothing to resemble the uniforms (or lack of uniforms) that they wore. She had boats loaded with soldiers coming to the land. It was an incredible work of art, and she was only nine at the time!

dough

A cooperative project the children can do is producing a play. We have a puppet show theater that our children thoroughly enjoy using. The children can make puppets that go along with the topic they are studying. Or they could just make up a play with the characters you already have.

a play

Your children could create a game show with questions that are relevant to the topic they are studying. It could be called something like, "Stump the Mom," or "Fool Father." This is a fun way to learn the facts about their topic.

a game show

Our current project is a family trivia game that the kids will give to relatives for Christmas. The children interviewed Grandma and Grandpa and the game will be about their childhood. They are researching major events that happened during their younger days. They will be creating memory cards, based on the memories of Grandma and Grandpa, but they will also be interspersing history cards, literature cards, etc. This project will take a lot of

family trivia game

preparation and much research. The final product, however, will be a family heirloom.

**family quilt**

If you like to sew, you could make a family quilt based on experiences in the life of your family.

**family newsletter**

If you did a unit on newspapers, you could begin a family newsletter. Your children could write letters to all the relatives asking them for stories about a particular area. If the first issue is on family pets, your children would ask the relatives to send in their favorite family pet stories, then the children would compile them and create a family newsletter. You might want to be careful with this one; the family might declare your children the official newsletter creators on a regular basis. Then again, that wouldn't be so bad, would it?

**the creation of a song**

One project could be the creation of a song to help memorize some facts. If they are trying to memorize the presidents of the United States, they could try to create a rhyming song with a catchy tune.

**a meal from that country**

If you are studying another country, you could have the children's project be a meal from that country. They would have to figure out what kind of food to make, how it is prepared, and if they can get the ingredients. Then, as a team, with the help of mom, they create an authentic dinner.

**Creating their own books**

Creating their own books, not to be confused with their notebook, also has a strong appeal to some of my children. If we're studying Pearl Harbor, they might create a book depicting the events of December 7, 1941.

While I'm working on this chapter right now, my son David is sitting behind me working on his own book. He is writing it for his younger brothers and sisters to enjoy. The process is even giving him spelling and handwriting practice.

**a diary**

Speaking of World War II, if you are currently studying the Holocaust, have your children write a diary in first person, as if they actually lived through the event. First, you might have them write from the perspective of a German soldier who is just following orders. You might have another child write from the perspective of a terrified German citizen, or a Holocaust victim. You might even choose to read them aloud on family night. This is a great way to deepen the understanding of history, and to strengthen creative writing skills.

Don't stop with just World War II events, though. Write diary entries from Civil War soldiers, Alamo fighters, Great Depression families, civil rights marchers, whalers, astronauts, presidents, or whomever you want your children to gain an in-depth understanding of. It really challenges them to think, explore, and process, while being fun all at the same time!

**General Tips on Projects:**

1. Projects really fuel in my children a desire to learn more about a subject. Encourage your children to discover new information to be used for their projects. Soon they won't want to base a project simply on what they already know, but will seek out resources to make their project as unique and interesting as they can.

2. When your children work on projects, you should set aside time for them to do the work. At our home, we have a block of time set aside in the afternoon for the children to work on their projects. Give your children that opportunity to give their project undivided attention.

3. I do not plan to do a project for every subject we study, and we usually cut back on the number of projects we do in the summertime, but the children will often do a project all on their own.

4. I often keep doing the same kinds of projects. That isn't too bad, but it's a good idea to try to come up with different types of projects. If "variety is the spice of life," imagine what it can do for education!

## FIRE BOOKS

The following suggestions for chapters are not "must do's," but simply suggestions. The purpose is to show you how to evaluate chapters you are reading and expand on them.

Whenever you use literature as a base for your children's education, you can discover for yourself the merit in each of the chapters. Take notes as you read, or read ahead before you read with the children. The latter suggestion takes more time, but will yield greater results. I almost always take notes as I'm reading. I don't have the time it takes to read each chapter first, but if that is a priority for you, you will love the results. We must rely on the Holy Spirit to guide us while we read. He will even use the children to help out. Sometimes one of the children will even point out something I have read, and say they would like to do that, or learn about that, or look that up.

Also, whenever you "do" something, there will almost always come another "something" to do. The following suggestions for chapters are not "must do's," but simply suggestions. The purpose is to show you how to evaluate chapters you are reading and expand on them.

I could turn almost every book I've read into a yearlong study. And yet, there is a time and place where we must simply read a book to our children as quickly as we can. You can then do some activities from the book for a few days or weeks. You must judge how your children are reacting to a book to decide how far you will go with it. There have been a couple of books that my children wanted me to read and read and read. We read well into our lunch hour. That's okay to do sometimes. One thing I really want to encourage you to do is listen to your children, to yourself, and to God. When you tell your children it is time to stop for the day and they all shout, "Keep reading," as they jump up and down, you probably should keep reading. We read *Nothing is Impossible* in three days. The children loved it so much that we just kept going. I will probably read it every couple of years.

I am not including these books here for you to follow to the letter, but for you to get an idea of what you can do with every book you read to your children.

Remember that while you read a book it can help you cover all the "subjects" on a continual basis—with the exception of math. You will need a math curriculum for that. But as you read the book, think about what areas of science, geography, art, history, etc., that the book reinforces. Don't get caught up, however, in the notion that you must do each subject each day. If you spend a few days or even a few weeks on science, you can spend a few days or weeks on geography. I've found that my children do not like to stop in the middle of a project to go on to something else. (Hmm? I wonder if they got that from me?) That may even be why I like this way of educating my children so much. I like to be able to finish something before I move on to the next thing.

## Carry On, Mr. Bowditch, by Jean Lee Latham

*Carry On, Mr. Bowditch*

I purchased my copy of *Carry On, Mr. Bowditch* at a library book sale for twenty-five cents. It saddens me that some of the best books around are being taken out of libraries and sold for pennies.

*Carry On, Mr. Bowditch* is the story of Nathaniel Bowditch, a man known as the father of navigation. It was his dedication to a subject and his love of learning that captured the mind of our children while reading this book. Well, perhaps it was the adventure too.

When I first began reading this book to my children, I didn't like the opening of the story and almost closed the book. As the first chapter title states, it begins with Nat making a wish. We don't believe in wish making in our house, so I did find that a bit offensive. I decided to read the first two chapters on my own first. I read them and fell in love with the book. I believe you will too.

### Chapter 1 The Good Luck Spell

See if your children can remember which war took place around 1775. You cannot do the Revolutionary War justice in one simple paper, or even in a short study of it. But you can do a few things. Or you can use this book as a part of your Revolutionary War study. Discuss how long the war lasted. Talk about the Declaration of Independence. Go further with this one if you want. But don't forget to come back to the book.

Using the index of an atlas, locate all the Salems in the United States. See if your children can figure out which Salem Nat was born in. You could talk about the Salem witch-hunts at this time with your older children.

Using the ages of all your children, come up with some math problems that will give an answer equal to their ages. You can do many math problems related to the ages of your children. You could add them all together. You could figure out the average age of your children, etc.

Try to find out what a shilling is. What would a shilling be worth today?

What's a towhead?

Have your children draw the picture in the book on page 4.

Measure all of your children. Have them stretch their arms out to their sides. Measure them from fingertip to fingertip. Compare it to their height. What is the average height? Graph the height and width (fingertip to fingertip) of your children.

What's a gable?

Have a physical challenge. See if your children can carry a shovel full of something heavy. See how far they can carry it without dropping its contents.

What is a new moon? Explore the phases of the moon.

**Chapter 2 The Privateers**
What is a fife?

Look up sloop, schooner, and square-rigger. See if you can find what the differences are. Draw one of them.

What's the difference between a privateer and a pirate ship?

Why would a sailor who's bad luck be called a Jonah? Read the book of Jonah in the Bible.

What's a wharf? Try to describe a wharf using the five senses.

What's a brig? And what's a binnacle list?

**Chapter 3 Word from the Pilgrim**
What else happened on April 19, 1775? Reenact the battle as best you can.

Play the floor game with some math facts. Try to do them quickly.

Find a recipe for ink. Get a quill. Write the alphabet using your ink recipe and a quill. Dust it with sand to dry the ink.

Where's Harvard? Why did Harvard begin?

What would it mean to "ballast his feet"?

What's an apothecary shop?

Write a paper about your hero.

## Chapter 4 Boys Don't Blubber
Where are the masts of a ship?

Have potatoes for breakfast, lunch, and dinner. Find recipes that include potatoes. See all the ways you can fix a potato. Discuss being frugal with food. Talk about the different products that are less expensive. Take a shopping trip to compare prices.

Talk about the items you purchase that are wants, rather than needs. What things could you do without if you didn't have very much money?

Who is Cornwallis?

See if you can find any information about Captain John Derby.

If it cost 1000 dollars for every dollar, how much would it cost for a loaf of bread? A gallon of milk? A pair of shoes? A new car? How much does it cost now for a bushel of corn? What's a bushel? What's a peck?

What can you find out about John Adams? When was he president of the United States?

Write a fictional story, based on the facts in the book, about the sinking of the *Polly*. First write out all the facts that you know about the *Polly*. Then add excitement, sights, and sounds. Jazz it up. This can be an individual effort or a combined storytelling time.

Have a shout-the-answer match. Mother, or someone else (if Mother has shouted quite enough already), shouts out questions, and the rest shout out the answers. Ask any kind of questions you want. Math questions, capitals, or other trivia would all be appropriate shoutings.

What does the term from "can-see to can't-see" mean? What term do we use now?

Go out and locate the Big Dipper, the North Star, etc. See what other constellations you can locate.

## Chapter 5 A Voice in the Night
Look up the word "garret."

What's a chandlery?

What does it mean to be indentured? Read *Benjamin Franklin* by Ingri and Edgar Parin D'Aulaire.

## Chapter 6 Sail by Ash Breeze
Draw a picture of what you think the garret looks like.

What's becalmed?

You might give a lesson here on the way our words can affect those around us.

Get a piece of wood (Log). Tie a string to it. Mark off every three feet with a yardstick. Now, drop the log and run as fast as you can until another person has counted to 10. When they yell stop, then stop running. Count how many knots you traveled. Do this several times and log your progress.

## Chapter 7 The Almanac
Look up surveying in the "cyclopedia."

Why do you suppose he put New England after Massachusetts?

See if you can get a hold of a theodolite. Perhaps a surveyor or county engineer would let you take a field trip to see surveying in action.

Find Cambridge on a map of Massachusetts.

Talk with your children about notebooks. Ask them what they would like to make notebooks about. This would be a good time to start them on their notebooks.

## Chapter 8 Lock, Stock, and Bookkeeper
Copy some of Washington's Rules of Civility in a copy notebook.

What did the flag look like at that time? What did the stars, stripes, and colors stand for? How big was the flag that was sewn by Betsy Ross?

Draw a picture of Washington riding into town on horseback. Try to find a picture that would resemble the scene to use as your base.

Find out information about Latin. Perhaps get your hands on the book *English From the Roots Up*. Learn as many Latin words as your children's interest allows. If it sparks, do it everyday.

Memorize John 1:1. Using dictionaries of various languages translate some of the key words of this verse.

Read a short biography on Isaac Newton.

Locate Russia, France, Spain, Bombay, and Calcutta on a map or globe.

## Chapter 9 Anchor to Windward
And how much prettier will Lizza be the following year?

Pass out the tissues!!!

## Chapter 10 Freedom
Find out about a steamship. Who invented the first one? What year was it invented?

Find other cases of words, or parts of words that are spelled alike but sound different.

Find the West Indies on a map

See if you can figure out how to tell time by the stars. Draw some Big Dippers in the night sky at different times. Go out for several nights at different times and tell what time it is.

Find Jamaica on a globe. Look it up in the "cyclopedia."

### Chapter 11 What Next?
What does the term "neutrality" mean?

Read something about Napoleon. Find a famous picture of him.

Who was the King of France?

Who is John Jay?

Find the Cape of Good Hope. See if you can find the origin of its name.

What is a sextant?

### Chapter 12 Down to the Sea
What's a slaver? What is its cargo? Why does Derby not want to be involved in it?

What's the dogwatch?

What's a binnacle?

What is a fo'c'sle?

If they get paid $12.00 a month, how much do they get paid per hour?

Look at the longitude and latitude lines on a globe. Create a treasure hunt using the lines as your key. Hide a pretend treasure, and then make a map for others to find it.

What is Polaris? What's a more common name for it?

Where is Bourbon? Track the sailing of the *Henry*. Start in Salem, go past the Cape of Good Hope, and land in Bourbon.

### Chapter 13 Discovery
What is a typhoon? What are the differences between a typhoon, a hurricane, a tornado, and a cyclone? See if you can find a satellite image of a typhoon. You might have to search the Internet for one.

See if you can find out any information about the livre. What is the French monetary system now? Can you find the exchange rate? Figure out how much money it would cost to buy a regular pair of shoes in France now.

What is meant by the term, "We'll beard Mr. Blunt of Newbury in his den"?

## Chapter 14 Nineteen Guns

Manila! Where is Manila? What are the latitude and longitude lines of Manila?

Define swarthy.

Find the Tagus River in Portugal. Find a photo of Lisbon.

Try to carry things on your head. Start with something small, like a book, then work up to trying to carry a laundry basket.

Find Funchal Bay

## Chapter 15 Sail, Hooooo

What's a squall?

Talk about the hemispheres. Build a model of the sun and the earth rotating around it.

Find the Indian Ocean.

What are the colors of the English and the French? Draw their flags. What is "The Union Jack"?

What is phosphorescence? What does the Greek word *phos* mean? Find other words beginning with *phos*. What do they have in common? If you live near one, take a trip to an old-fashioned soda fountain and order a phosphate.

Where is the sun's zenith?

Draw the picture at the end of the chapter.

## Chapter 16 A Simple Matter of Mathematics

Draw the canoe based on the description in the book. Don't forget the laughing natives.

What is a league?

Find Cape Ann.

### Chapter 17 Lunars and Moonlight
Research the beginning of the American navy. What year did it begin? How many ships were involved? Can you find the builder of the ships?

Write the quote, "Mathematics is nothing if it isn't correct!"

Write down all the definitions of the word "signature."

How many feet is the moon's diameter?

Discover something about the Barbary pirates.

### Chapter 18 The *Astrea* to the Rescue
Where is Cadiz?

What is a promontory?

Find the Nile.

Pass out the tissues!

### Chapter 19 Strange Sailing Orders
What is a dowry?

What is "consumption"?

Where is Batavia?

### Chapter 20 Book Sailing
What is a monsoon? When is the monsoon season in Manila?

### Chapter 21 Sealing is Safer

What's a marlinespike? What did she mean by "cut her teeth"?

Get a knot book from the library or look in a Boy Scout handbook and learn some knots. Is it right to spell the word cookie, cooky? What other words end in i.e. like cookie? Can you spell those words with a y?

**Chapter 22 Science and Sumatra**
Where did the quote, "A prophet is without honor in his own country," come from?

How do you "sit alone in a crowd"? Write a paper on sitting alone in a crowd.

What is betel?

**Chapter 23 Captain Bowditch Commanding**
Look up Sumatra and the Pepper Islands.

Find out everything you can about coral reefs.

What is a sarong?

How much is a picul?

What would be a "mirthless" smile?

**Chapter 24 Man Against the Fog**
Enjoy the last chapter!

From here my children decided they wanted to know more about Napoleon. Although I had intended to go somewhere else, the spark was ignited to learn about Napoleon and France. So that is where we went.

*Nothing is Impossible*

**<u>Nothing is Impossible by Dorothy Aldis</u>**
*Nothing is Impossible* is the story of Beatrix Potter. If you are just beginning with the idea of using notebooks to educate your children, this book will be a great start to help your children under-

stand what they can do with notebooks.

**Chapter 1: Locked up tight**
With the older children you could have them write a paper about some of their earliest memories. Younger children can dictate to you what they remember from times past.

With the little children, you can quickly say their numbers, one through ten, then quickly count backwards.

Look up London in the encyclopedia, on a globe, and on a flat map or atlas.

There are many pictures your children can draw from this chapter. You could have them draw what it would look like from the nursery window, looking down on the street. You could have them draw the various servants, or even draw a lonely girl in her bedroom. Most of the time, I don't direct my children to draw a specific scene. That often limits their desire to learn. However, I will sometimes show them a picture, let's say a picture of the city of London. I will show it to them for a couple of minutes, allowing them to study it for a short time. Then I will remove the picture and have them draw it from memory. When they have completed their drawing, I will then allow them to once again view the picture and critique their own picture. If they choose, they are then allowed to draw the picture while looking at it.

Look up the word "perambulator," after speculating what it might mean.

Talk about the lamplighter. You could branch out here into a little talk about electricity.

See if you can discover what kind of birds would fly around London.

Separate your day by activities rather than the clock. What activities do you do every day? You could also do this with the week if you do different things on different days. This is a good way to teach the days of the week to your younger children. You could say something like, "The first day of the week is Sunday. We go to church on the first day of the week. Next comes Monday. We again sit down and do our schoolwork, etc. I've found the more I can personalize my child's learning, the more they get out of it.

Make rice pudding for lunch. You could even make a veal dish for dinner if you'd like. Veal Parmesan is a big hit with children. Some people have trouble with the thought of eating veal, so as with any suggestion here, you can just skip it.

Discover something about the röyalty of London.

Take a walk with your children. Take along with you a nature notebook, colored pencils, and a book on flowers. See how many flowers you can discover on your walk. Draw them into your nature notebook.

Try drawing a fox with gloves.

## Chapter 2: An Upsetting Morning
You could use this chapter as a precursor to a study on "how life begins." You will have to determine on your own if your children are at an age of learning about where babies come from. I didn't do a lot of activities with this chapter.

## Chapter 3: A Strange Half Hour
Do a study on mice. Draw them. You could even make a mouse house out of a box.

Create some rhyming names. Try to rhyme the children's names.

Tell your children a story about your family. Have Daddy tell a story about his family. Do a family tree.

Look up "barrister" in the dictionary.

Play a game of hide-and-seek.

Have teatime with your children. Have them get dressed up in their finest clothing. Make cookies, biscuits, or scones. Prepare a tea that children like. Mine tend to like apple cinnamon the best. Have fun with it. Let them choose what kind of tea they want. You could prepare everything ahead of time and read this chapter while you are having tea. Teatime is a good time to read poetry or the Psalms with each other. It is also a good time to tell "family" stories. You could encourage your children to tell stories about themselves. You could have each of them choose something they want to read to each other. They could even have an original poem they would like to read. Teatime is a marvelous time! It could become tradition long after you finish *Nothing is Impossible*.

What is whist?

Discover all you can about the Puritans. See if you can find any information about Puritans who stayed in England. What became of them?

What is treason?

What is a spinning wheel?

**Chapter 4 Why are you so frightened?**
Who is Tennyson? Find something he wrote and copy it into a notebook.

Look up mushrooms. Draw a mushroom or two. Go mushroom hunting. Have your children decide where they think the mushrooms will be. Be sure to make it perfectly clear they aren't to even touch them without thoroughly washing their hands afterwards.

Look up taxidermy. See if you can visit a taxidermist or a place that would have "stuffed" animals. I've heard that Cabella's (the sporting goods store) has a lot. You could take a trip to a natural history museum.

**Chapter 5 Country Holidays**
Draw a map of England. Find Liverpool and London and place them on the map.

Spend some time having your children think about the things they have in common with each other. Concentrate on the siblings that have a harder time getting along with each other. Assign them a task to do that they both like. For example, if they both like to draw, give them an assignment to draw together.

Find how far it is from London to Scotland. You could do some calculations about how long it would take to go from London to Scotland via different modes of transportation. For example, they would have taken a horse-drawn carriage going twenty miles per hour, etc. You could calculate how long it would take in a plane now. Go a little further and talk about the countryside they would miss by taking a plane. Find out some interesting information about Scotland.

Write a letter to a friend or relative. Make it as neat as possible. If there are errors, rewrite the letter.

Have your older children think of something they could teach one of their younger siblings. Have them do it.

Make a flower press.

Talk about the passing of time. Discuss the importance of not being idle. Talk about the different things in their life that pass time quickly and the things that seem to drag time on.


**Chapter 6 A Peculiar Winter**
Get out the paints and paint something.

Do a little research on the health benefits of honey.

What is meant by the term, "building up his constitution"?

Locate the town of Wray, England.

Practice some spelling words. Have the children try to picture the word in their mind.

Dance and sing a couple of songs.

Draw the insides of an animal. Locate their bones, stomach, and heart.

Draw a flower. Locate and label the stamen and the pistil. Feel free to locate other parts as well.

Look up pollen in the encyclopedia or on the Internet. See if you can find some information that you had never known before.

Give your child a geranium, two snails, and a worm. Or, just a geranium if you wish. You could gather some worms or night-crawlers and start a "farm." See what you can discover about worms from the local library.

## Chapter 7 Beatrix and Bertrum are Free

Design a castle. Little kids can make a simple design; older children should be able to make a basic floor plan to scale using graph paper. Or you could have the children create a castle out of blocks or Legos while you read the story.

Eat fish for dinner. Or fish sticks (if you must).

Discover all you can about fish. How do they breathe? What kinds of fish are in the lakes, rivers, and streams in your area? Draw a skeleton of a fish. Go fishing if you can.

Write a poem about fishing. If you've never been fishing, talk to someone who has been fishing and have him relay his favorite fishing story.

Learn about bats. You will want to skip the part of the millions and millions of years. (I'm going to add in here that you, as the parent, have a responsibility to your children to siphon out information that you do not want them to know. Or, use the moment to explain your beliefs. It is allowed to skip parts of a book.) Or this may be an opportune time to discuss the erroneous idea that the earth is millions of years old.

Discover some information about caves. Learn about the different formations within a cave.

Look up "turreted" in the dictionary. Perhaps draw a new castle that is turreted.

See what you can discover about "the Lake District." Can you find out about any famous people who once lived there?

Take a walk in *your* countryside. Try to point out as many trees, flowers, and weeds as you can. Of course, you might need to take a field guide with you. Or better yet, try to arrange a guided tour of a nearby nature reserve with the local conservation office. Don't forget to take your nature notebook so you can draw many of the plants that you discover along the way.

Take a library trip and check out all the books on mushrooms.

Make up a story about some field mice that live under a mushroom.

Discover your child's scientific name. Have your children tell you what they are most interested in learning, then find out what the scientific name is for that particular area. If you have a son who thinks football is the area of his greatest interest, you could call him a podiosphereologist. Use a thesaurus if you need help coming up with a good word for each of the children. You could explain, if you haven't already, how many of our words come from Latin derivatives. They might have fun discovering all sorts of "new" words for common items around the house. Give them ample time to play with the thesaurus.

Get some clay and try to make models of animals. See if you can make some of them life-size. Paint them if you wish.

**Chapter 8 The Best Time of All**
Have your children begin writing in a journal. I can tell you from experience that if you don't remind them each day, they will more than likely forget to do it. Perhaps you could even set aside a few minutes of each day for them to work in their journals. You know, this wouldn't be a bad idea for Mom either. If you have a child that is not of writing age yet, have him dictate to you what he would like written. You could choose a sentence or a couple of words and use them for his handwriting practice. If you can afford to, purchase a hardbound journal for your children to write in, or you can have them use a composition book. Don't get them a five-year diary. There isn't enough room to write more than a couple of sentences in each spot.

Get out a microscope and look in it. Have the children gather all sorts of things to view. This may take you several days. Have them draw what they see.

Look up hedgehog in the encyclopedia.

**Chapter 9 The Nicest Boy**
Study the work of some famous painters. Look up the work of Van Dyck. Allow your children to look at a picture for a few minutes. Then remove the picture and have them draw or paint what they can remember from the painting. After they are finished allow them to once again see the picture. Have them then try to paint or draw the picture again.

Take the children who are old enough to an art gallery. Talk about the great works of art. Decide what kinds of paintings you like and what kinds you don't. Discuss the different types of paintings.

**Chapter 10 Annie Carter Takes Charge**
Have your kids try the German phrases.

Go ahead! Sing the German song.

What does "eccentric" mean?

**Chapter 11 The Years Go Marching On**
Visit a place with animals. Perhaps it could be a zoo, a farm, or even your own backyard. Allow them to spend a decent amount of time watching one group of animals. Then have them describe the animals. This is a lesson in description, so if you want them to add more adjectives, tell them you want more.

Another lesson would be to show the children the same picture. On a piece of paper have them list five words to describe the picture. Now read the words aloud and see if the words are the same. An abstract picture may work best for this exercise.

Read a short story about snails.

What is rheumatic fever?

Discover the falcon. What is a Barbary falcon?

What is botany?

How would you go about painting the smell of heather? Could you "paint" the smell of heather with words?

What's a bungalow?

Read about Queen Victoria.

What is a jackdaw?

**Chapter 12 A Letter to Noel**
Make up a story. Together with the children, decide what characters will be in the story. You could discuss a little about their particular characteristics. Don't decide too many details, however,

as that will not allow for as much creativity from the children.

Read the real *The Tale of Peter Rabbit* to your children. Be sure to show them the wonderful illustrations.

Read a little Shakespeare to the children to give them a feel for it. If they like, let them act out one of the plays.

### Chapter 13 A Bell: Ding Dong
Figure out how much 14 pounds would be worth in dollars today.

Go to a colorful place with a palette of paints and try to mix the colors to create just the color you want. Use them on a canvas if you'd like.

SMILE! This chapter is delightful.

### Chapter 14 No Santa Claus That Year
Pass out tissues to the children before you begin reading this chapter.

Read *The Tailor of Gloucester* to your children.

Learn the characteristics of the great horned owl. There is a wonderful series of books put out by ATI, called *Character Traits*. These have marvelous illustrations of many animals. "The Great Horned Owl" was especially enlightening to us.

After reading of the demise of Hunca, use your tissues and cry hysterically.

Save your tissues—you will need them at the end of the chapter.

### Chapter 15 A New Beginning
Read *The Tale of Jeremy Fisher*.

Locate Sawrey in England.

Use the indented paragraph on page 133 as a piece of copy work. It is simply delightful.

Look at the illustrations in *The Tale of Tom Kitten, The Tale of*

*Jemima Puddleduck*, and *The Roly-Poly Pudding* to get an idea of what it was like at Hill Top.

Look up all the Scriptures you can find relating to sheep.

**Chapter 16 A Wonderful Decision**
Look up the heart and its function in a science encyclopedia. Create a model of the heart.

Bake a cake for dinner.

**Chapter 17 What Happened Later**
Gather all the Beatrix Potter books you can find. Sit down with some tea and crumpets or scones and read them all!

When we finished this book, I had to do some household chores. When I returned to the living room, our darling Ashley was sitting on the couch with all of our children surrounding her. Little Erica, all of eighteen months, sat on her lap. Briana cozied up next to her. John was on her other side, getting closer and closer to her as I watched. David and Cathy sat at her feet, and Christi stood behind peering at the book in her hands. Ashley was about twelve at the time. In her best little English accent, this is what she read, "I am sorry to say that Peter was not very well during the evening. His mother put him to bed, and made some chamomile tea; and she gave a dose of it to Peter! One table-spoonful to be taken at bed-time. But Flopsy, Mopsy, and Cottontail had bread and milk and blackberries, for supper. The End."

And all the children clapped!

# FURTHER INFORMATION

There are many great books on the shelves at the library and available from various sources. There are also several books available that give a book list for you to choose the proper books for your children. Rather than duplicate the efforts that have already been made, I will offer just a few of our favorites. My criterion for a great Fire book is this: it must have many sparks within the pages. In other words, it must prompt my children to want to know more about some of the things that are mentioned in the book.

> My criterion for a great Fire book is this: it must have many sparks within the pages.

*Johnny Tremain* is a book that is often listed on my children's all-time favorite list. They loved hearing about Johnny. This book is set during the Revolutionary War. It is a great Fire book.

> *Johnny Tremain*

Another fabulous Fire book is *Amos Fortune, Free Man*. This is the story of a slave who desires to be free. This book did more for my children than any course they could have taken on racial tolerance.

> *Amos Fortune, Free Man*

*Cheaper By the Dozen* is a book based on the life of the Gilbreath family. Mr. Gilbreath really taught his children a lot and I have stolen some of my ideas from him. During their summer vacation at "the shoe," Mr. Gilbreath wrote out the entire Morse code in black paint on the walls of their home. Look out, Home Interiors! Here comes a homeschooling parent. This book was positively delightful. There were some parts I had to skip when reading this book aloud.

> *Cheaper By the Dozen*

Books on the life of George Washington Carver are wonderful. We read several books on his life one month. One of the things we discovered when doing this is that not all books have all the facts right. It was quite amazing to us. But, all was not lost. We decided we must discover the truth. So we did more research on his life than I had originally anticipated.

> George Washington Carver

*Vinegar Boy* by Alberta Hawse, and *The Bronze Bow* by Elizabeth Speare were both loved, and inspired our children to want to delve further into the time period around the life of our Lord. They were both powerful books. You *cannot* miss them!

> *Vinegar Boy*
> *The Bronze Bow*

I have personally found biographies to be the greatest Fire books. You can pretty much know you're lighting fires if you are reading biographies.

If you get stumped about what to do next, pick up a good biography and begin reading. Follow the Lord and watch your children. You will know where to go next.

I have created a Web site devoted to refreshing, encouraging, and uplifting the homeschool parent. It can be found at www.ignitethefire.com .

In addition I also have an E-mail loop for parents who use the Fire Philosophy to educate their children. Many ideas on the loop are not found in the pages of this book. You can find firetime by going to www.yahoogroups.com and doing a search for "firetime."

Weekly I write a column at www.homeschool.crosswalk.com . The home school channel on Crosswalk is one of the best homeschool sites on the Internet!

If you would like to contact me, you may do so by writing to terri@ignitethefire.com .

# INDEX

## 2

2 Cor. 3:17, 10

## 3

**3 ring binders, 58**
3 x 5 cards, 30

## A

a diary, 69
a game show, 68
a meal from that country, 69
**a movie, 43**
a play, 68
**Animals, 63**
Art Notebook, **50**
**assemble a book, 35**

## B

**Balloons, 64**
**Bible, 58**
**Biographies, 34**
**Biography, 41**
**Black markers, 62**
**board game, 34**
**board games, 42**
**Book, 45**
**BOOKS/library card, 61**

## C

**Car keys, 64**
Carry On, Mr. Bowditch, 72
color-coded memorization., 28
**Composition books, 59**
**Contest, 40**
**Contests, 34,** 68
**Cookbook, 64**
**Correspond, 36**
create something, 67
Creating their own books, 69
Cuisenaire rods, 63

## D

Deuteronomy 6:5-9, 11
dough, 68
Duct tape, 59

## E

"Education is not the filling of a bucket, but the lighting of a fire." William Butler Yeats., 8

# N

# O

# P

# R

# S

# T

## Uncommon Courtesy

Let's face up to the fact that "common courtesy" isn't as common as it used to be! Proper etiquette is practically extinct. Uncommon Courtesy for Kids teaches children 56 ways to be considerate of others. It will help your children understand what to do and what not to do in eleven different situations. This kit covers everything from meal times to going to church. Includes a laminated list of all 56 rules, a reproducible coloring book, and individual posters for each rule. For ages 3 and up.
Item #1799.........$14⁹⁵

## Rules For Young Friends

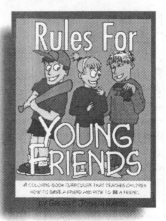

Do you feel overrun by your child's playmates? This valuable resource provides 11 simple rules for friendships. Rules For Young Friends is a coloring book curriculum that will help you teach your child to be a good host and a good guest. In addition to family house rules, this set includes rules for loyalty towards family members, borrowing and loaning toys, friends who interrupt chores and much more. This training kit has worked for thousands of families, and it can work for you.
Item #1042.........$14⁹⁵

## The Choreganizer

Overwhelmed by household chores at your house? *The Choreganizer* to the rescue! This valuable tool helps you: **1) Identify all the household chores that need to be done** (with 60 colorful chore cards). **2) Assign them to your children** (on individualized chore charts) and **3) Monitor completion on a daily basis.** Visually appealing and fun to use, it also offers its unique **Chore Store, Mom Money** and **Dad Dollars** giving your children tangible goals to work toward and a way for you to say "thanks for helping."
Item #1725.........$16⁹⁵

## WILL YOUR CHILD BE A FOLLOWER OR A LEADER?

Dr. Jeff Myers has found that people who communicate well are chosen to be leaders. His new book *From Playpen to Podium* shows you how to improve your child's communication skills through reading, writing and thinking skills. It also enhances their comfort in social situations, helps them resist negative peer influences, and develops leadership skills. Now you can easily give your children the communication advantage.

Item #1036.........$14⁹⁵

**AVAILABLE THROUGH YOUR LOCAL BOOKSTORE OR BY CALLING 1-800-225-5259**

## The Original 21 Rules of this House

"In this house we obey the Lord Jesus Christ" So begin 21 house reles for good behavior that have transformed thousands of Christian families. Who would have thought that 95% of all the trouble children normally get into could be dealt with so effectively in just 21 rules? The kit comes complete with a "Jelly Proof" master list, a coloring book illustrating all 21 rules. individual rule posters to focus on each rule and instructions for using the kit with your family.

**Item #1041......$14⁹⁵**

## SEARCHING FOR TREASURE

Searching for Treasure provides 20 weeks of daily Bible lessons from the book of Proverbs. Each lesson is age-integrated so the entire family can learn and grow together. Specifically designed to build character, Searching for Treasure will have an effect on your family immediately. Topics include choosing your friends, honoring parents, giving up your pride, overcoming temptation, gossiping, seeking revenge, being generous, working hard, and numerous others. Each lesson includes several different verses to read, a memory verse, discussion questions, and teaching tips for the parents. A fold-out game board and memory-verse cards are included to make teaching the program simple for the parents and exciting for the kids. Searching for Treasure can be used for Sunday School, home school, Bible Clubs, and children's ministries of all kinds.

**Item #1760......$19⁹⁵**

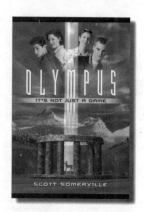

Got a new reader or two? What better way to get your youngreaders reading for pleasure than an action-packed adventure novel? And what better topic than the futures most popular web-based computer game, Olympus? And what better heroes to identify with than a family of Christian home-schoolers off to rescue a neighbor's runaway teenager from a web of virtual-reality high-tech game designers and corrupt children's services officials? It's all here in one cliff-hanger after another. The novel is also a clear warning to teens not to let their computer game playing get out of hand! (Scott Somerville sees what is coming in the next few years in virtual-reality games and it is not just a game!). Our family stayed up until 1:00 A.M. for several nights because my children couldn't bear to let Sano and I stop reading aloud. Recommended for all ages with parental discretion due to a few intense conflicts between good and evil. If you enjoy C.S. Lewis' Chronicles of Namia, and Space Trilogy, you'll love Olympus.

**Item #8502.......$14⁹⁵**

## Classics at Home

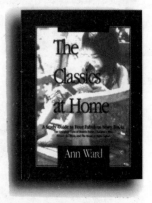

Ann Ward has done it again! This fabulous study guide is broken up into daily lessons that include reading assignments from several classic children's stories, vocabulary words from the reading assignment, questions to exercise your child's comprehension ability, and Bible verses dealing with the theme presented in the assigned story. In The classics at Home, Ann Ward will lead you through The complete Tales of Beatrix Potter, Charlotte's Web, Winnie the Pooh, and The House at Pooh Corner.

**Item #1736.......$19⁹⁵**